Healing Body & Soul

Also by John A. Sanford

MINISTRY BURNOUT

Healing

Body & Soul

The Meaning of Illness in the
New Testament
and in Psychotherapy

John A. Sanford

Gracewing
Leominster, England

Westminster/John Knox Press
Louisville, Kentucky

First published in the British Commonwealth in 1992 by Gracewing, Southern Avenue, Leominster HR6 0QF, England

First published in the United States in 1992 by Westminster/John Knox Press, 100 Witherspoon Street, Louisville, Kentucky 40202-1396

© 1992 John A. Sanford

Book design by Kevin Raquepaw

This book is printed on recycled acid-free paper that meets the American National Standards Institute Z39.48 standard. ∞

PRINTED IN THE UNITED STATES OF AMERICA
2 4 6 8 9 7 5 3 1

British Cataloging-in-Publication Data

A catalogue record for this book is available from the British Library.

ISBN 0-852-44228-9

Library of Congress Cataloging-in-Publication Data

Sanford, John A.
  Healing body and soul : the meaning of illness in the New Testament and in psychotherapy / John A. Sanford. — 1st ed.
      p.   cm.
  ISBN 0-664-25351-2 (pbk. : alk. paper)
  1. Healing in the Bible.   2. Medicine in the Bible.   3. Spiritual healing—Biblical teaching.   4. Psychotherapy—Religious aspects—Christianity.   5. Bible.   N.T.—Criticism, interpretation, etc.
  I. Title.
BS2545.H4S36   1992
261.8'321—dc20   92-12730

Contents

88250

Introduction

The seeds of my lifelong interest in spiritual and psychological healing were sown early in my life, for both my father and mother were leaders in the spiritual healing movement. My father, the Rev. Edgar L. Sanford, an Episcopal minister, had an active program of pastoral work and counseling in his churches; later in life, he wrote a book on pastoral care. My mother, the late Agnes Sanford, became well known in the spiritual healing field and wrote many books on the subject, a number of which are still in print. My own personality is religious by nature, and in my early twenties I decided to follow the footsteps of my father (and grandfathers as well) and entered seminary to prepare to be an Episcopal minister. However, in my second year of seminary I fell into a state of anxiety so acute that I was forced to abandon school and find help. I must have gone to a dozen different people of all sorts of professional persuasions, but no one seemed able to help me. Somewhat in despair, I left the East Coast for the West to make my living as a surveyor—a trade I had picked up quite early in life—and in Los Angeles continued my search for someone to help me. It was there that I was directed by an Episcopal chaplain to Fritz Kunkel. I had read Kunkel's books while in seminary and had been greatly impressed by his unique combination of psychological insight and scriptural knowledge. So I contacted Kunkel, who agreed to see me, and two minutes into our first conversation together I knew this was the man who could help me. Since then, my own healing process has developed into a lifework involving both the psychological and spiritual dimensions of healing.

Out of this kind of interest and background has come this book, which is built around three important New Testament themes: the spiritual meaning of illness as seen in the various healing stories of the Gospels, the connection between faith and knowledge in the healing process, and the New Testament teachings about the health of the soul. These areas of concern will be dealt with in three ways: first, each will be approached as a New Testament study; second, each will be related to contemporary concerns regarding illness and health; and third, although this is not a self-help book as such, from time to time some practical recommendations will be made about how we can apply the biblical admonitions to our own lives.

Because I am a Jungian analyst, it is natural that I should utilize some concepts from Jungian psychology in my interpretation of the biblical healing stories. For the reader who is not familiar with this psychological language, I will here introduce the most important psychological terms and concepts.

Both Jung and Kunkel believed in the human *psyche.* The word "psyche" refers to personality in its largest possible sense. The totality of the human personality, conscious and unconscious, is the psyche. Jung and Kunkel also believed that the psyche has not one center, as is believed in most psychologies, but two. First, there is the lesser center of the *ego*. The word "ego" means "I" in Greek and may be roughly defined as the center of the conscious personality. Thus the ego is that part of ourselves with which we are most identified. The *Self*, on the other hand, is the center of the total personality. The Self is sometimes referred to by Kunkel as the "Real Self" to distinguish it from the false idea many of us have about ourselves. The word "Center" may be used synonymously with the word "Self." Each of these three phrases—Self, Real Self, and Center—expresses in its own way the idea that beyond our limited conscious personality there is a larger personality that includes both the ego and that greater personality to which we belong, of which we are largely unaware.

The Bible also speaks of a personality larger than the ego. When Paul, for instance, said to the Galatians, "It is no longer I who live, but Christ who lives in me" (Gal. 2:20), he was expressing the mystery of the two centers of the personality. The fact that he said Christ lived in him shows the closeness between the Self and God. In fact, Jung said the idea of God emerges spontaneously from the Self, which is like an *imago dei*, an image of God, that lives within our very souls. For this reason, the early Christian philosopher Tertullian once said that the soul was by nature Christian, because the soul was the dwelling place of the divine Logos, or Christ.

This brings us to the *soul*. Although it is a biblical word rather than a contemporary psychological term, it is irreplaceable because it expresses nuances of meaning that elude more conventional terms. In the New Testament, the word "soul" refers to our innermost essence from which emerges our affective, creative, emotional life. It is also this mysterious soul of ours that is said to live on after the death of the body if raised to new life in Christ. Yet the soul is not by nature immortal. It can become corrupted and perish; it lives on only if it has become enlightened. Danish novelist Isak Dinesen once said of dreams that they were like smells because both refuse to yield up their innermost meaning to words. The same is true of the soul, which though it refuses to allow its essence to be caught in a net of words, is essential in any religious psychology.

Ordinarily, however, the ego knows little or nothing of the soul or of the larger Self. It is as though the ego lives behind a huge stone barricade and is unaware that there is anything on the other side. The ego thus lives in a state of unconsciousness. Everything that we do not know about ourselves is called *the unconscious,* simply because we are unaware of it. Many of the things we do not know about ourselves stem from our personal history. For instance, perhaps troublesome or traumatic episodes in our childhood have been so deeply repressed that we no longer recall them. These episodes of which we are no longer aware constitute the *personal unconscious.* But there is also a much larger area of the unconscious that Jung called the *collective unconscious.* This amounts to something like a historical memory—as if the pooled psychological and spiritual history of the human race lived on in each of us in a mind a million years old. This is the collective unconscious, and it is here that the Self is to be found.

A simple diagram will represent schematically the psychological structure we have been discussing.

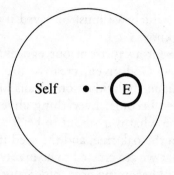

In this diagram the larger circle and the dot both represent the Self or Center, for the Self is both the totality of the personality (represented by the circle) and its center (represented by the dot). The smaller circle represents the ego, and the thick line around it represents the wall around the ego, a wall which to a certain extent the ego must have in order to preserve its self-identity and its capacity for independent psychological functioning. But if the wall is excessively thick, it represents an ego that has become so enclosed that it is impervious to creative influences from the Self and shut off from viable relationships with other people. Sometimes the excessive thickness of the wall is the result of childhood injuries, but it is also an all-too-natural state of affairs that our conscious life should be enclosed in a small psychic space. This thick wall around us limits and impoverishes our personality and leads to what Kunkel called our *egocentricity:* the narcissistic state in which we live out of our narrow ego and are concerned only, or mostly, with our own egocentric defenses and ambitions. Unless this egocentric barrier against the Self is broken down, the larger life of the Self cannot come into us. Psychologically, the egocentric state corresponds to the religious notion of original sin, for it is a state of affairs from which we must be saved if we are to live creatively and know God.

This movement away from our egocentricity and toward the larger, God-given, creative life of the Self is called *individuation*. Individuation means becoming what we are meant to become. Everything alive in this world seeks to become what it is meant to be: The acorn strives to develop into the oak tree, and the seed into the wheat. To become what we are created to be involves us necessarily in a process of becoming psychologically and spiritually conscious. It is a process that the New Testament described, in its own way, long before modern psychology came upon the scene. It is to this that we now turn.

1

The Meaning of Illness
in the Gospels
and in Psychotherapy Today

Illness, and the suffering that comes from it, affects us all. There is no one among us who has not been touched by illness; some live with it on a daily basis. We also suffer because of the illnesses of those whom we love, and, of course, in the end we will all die, many as a result of illness.

Faced by the specter of illness and suffering, the human spirit struggles to find a meaning in it. Does illness have a meaning? If so, what is its message to us? Or is illness a meaningless event in a life that is also devoid of meaning, an unfortunate occurrence in a world in which life and death, health and illness vie with each other with no apparent meaning or purpose behind them? Will certain attitudes toward illness help us recover, or is there nothing we can do spiritually in the face of illness except endure it as best we can? These are questions and issues with which thinking people struggle. Such struggle is all the more likely to occur if we are believers—or want to be believers—in God, for if there is a divine power at work in the world, what is the relationship of illness to this power? Does God send illness upon us? Does God ever intend for us to be ill? Is God concerned when we are ill?

The theologian has long wrestled with these questions and issues, but the psychotherapist* is also concerned with them, for the psychotherapist works with people who are ill in spirit and sometimes in body as well. To help her patient,[1] the therapist must aid him in coming to terms with the illness besetting him. If there is a meaning in the illness, it needs to be found. If there is no meaning, the patient needs help in dealing with that harsh reality as well. Such issues in psychotherapy are by no means merely intellectual ones, for the attitude we have toward our illness may either facilitate or hinder our recovery.

These are some of the issues with which we will deal in our exploration of the meaning of illness. In this endeavor we will examine certain current beliefs regarding the meaning of illness and explore the psychology of individuation as set forth by C. G. Jung and Fritz Kunkel. But mostly we will look to the Bible as a source of guidance, beginning with the story of the healing of the man born blind.

The Story of the Man Born Blind

As he [Jesus] went along, he saw a man who had been blind from birth. His disciples asked him, 'Rabbi, who

---

*By psychotherapy I mean any ongoing therapeutic work of a psychological or spiritual nature, or both, in which one person functions as the healer and the other is the client or patient. Thus in this volume "psychotherapist" can refer to a psychologist, pastoral counselor, psychiatrist, marriage and family counselor, and so on.

sinned, this man or his parents, for him to have been born blind?' 'Neither he nor his parents sinned,' Jesus answered 'he was born blind so that the works of God might be displayed in him.

'As long as the day lasts
I must carry out the work of the one who sent me;
the night will soon be here when no one can work.
As long as I am in the world
I am the light of the world.'

Having said this, he spat on the ground, made a paste with the spittle, put this over the eyes of the blind man, and said to him, 'Go and wash in the Pool of Siloam (a name that means 'sent'). So the blind man went off and washed himself, and came away with his sight restored. (John 9:1–7, JB)

This story contains many interesting points. The author of the fourth Gospel[2] typically tells a story at the beginning of a section and then uses the story as a springboard from which to launch into an intricate theological pronouncement or discussion. In the case of John 9, the story of the healing of the man born blind leads to a discussion of "seeing" and "not seeing" in a spiritual sense. However, to explore this dimension of meaning in the story would lead us beyond our present purposes; we will concentrate only on the light the story throws on the meaning of illness and health.

Let's begin with some instructive details. First is the means Jesus uses to effect a cure, in this case the use of a kind of ointment or salve compounded from ordinary dirt and Jesus' spittle. Why such a strange method of healing? It is certainly a humble way in which to be healed. We do not hear that Jesus took the blind man to the top of a great mountain and performed an awe-inspiring ceremony to heal him. To the contrary, he healed him with mundane mud and spit. What cured the man was something earthy and humble, and it left him with no room for an inflated ego.

Second, while the healing process was initiated when Jesus anointed the man's eyes with spittle, it was not effected until the man went to the Pool of Siloam and washed his eyes with its water. Scholars see a not-so-hidden significance in the word "Siloam," which means, as John himself tells us, "sent," pointing out that Jesus is the one sent by God. But in addition we can note that for the blind man to be healed, he himself had to do something about it; he did not passively receive his sight but had to make a pilgrimage to this pool. This matter of seeking out healing or making a pilgrimage, to which we will return later, is an important theme in healing.

Third, we note the use of a body fluid for the purpose of healing. This idea, which sounds strange to us, is more understandable when we recall the way the ancient mind thought of the relationship of soul and body. Today most people believe that the life of the body somehow engenders what we call personality or soul; therefore, if the body dies, the personality also dies, or so it is commonly believed. For the ancient mind, however, it was the other way around: It was the soul that enlivened the body, and when the soul departed from the body (which it did with the final breath), then the body died, for now its life force was gone.

In ancient times, many people believed the soul resided in the body fluids, especially in the blood, which seemed to permeate the whole body as it was supposed the soul permeated the body. The ancient connection between blood and life-essence is the reason Christians believe they are saved by the blood of Christ; it is also why the partaker of the Eucharist believes in the sanctifying power of the wine, which symbolizes—or perhaps actually *is*—the blood of Christ. We can suppose, therefore, that when Jesus healed the man born blind by the use of spittle, he was conveying to that man his own life-essence.

The word for "washing" used in the story also carries a nuance of meaning that would escape the reader of an English translation but that is apparent in the Greek. The Greeks had three words for washing. The first, *plynō,* meant to wash things, such as garments. The second, *louō,* was used with reference to washing the whole body. The third, *niptō,* referred to the washing of a part of the body. In John's story, the word *niptō* is used because the man needs to wash only his eyes. If Jesus had believed that the man's blindness was the result of his sinfulness, he probably would have used the word *louō,* for this word, referring as it did to a total washing, also implied a ritual cleansing. The fact is, as we will soon note, Jesus did not believe the man's blindness was the result of his sin. This is why he told him to bathe only his eyes (*niptō*) instead of washing his entire body (*louō*).

Other people, however, had a different opinion, for the disciples asked Jesus, "Rabbi, who sinned, this man or his parents, for him to have been born blind?" In fact, the ancient Hebrews believed illness resulted from sin. This belief rested on the premise that all things, good or ill, come from Yahweh. Consider, for example, the words of God according to Isaiah:

> I am Yahweh, and there is no other,
> I form the light and I create the darkness,

> I make well-being, and I create disaster,
> I, Yahweh, do all these things.
> (Isa. 45:7, NJB. See also Amos 3:6, 3:38)

The Old Testament has what can be called an unflinching monotheism. By this I mean that the religious geniuses of the Old Testament era were so devoted to monotheism that they ascribed to God everything that happened, for which reason there was virtually no mention made in the Old Testament of a devil.[3]

This belief that everything came from God included illness. The thinking was that because God was just, God would not send illness upon a person unless that person deserved it.[4] Consider, for instance, this lament:

> Yahweh, do not correct me in anger,
> do not discipline me in wrath.
> For your arrows have pierced deep into me,
> your hand has pressed down upon me.
> Your indignation has left no part of me unscathed,
> my sin has left no health in my bones.
>
> My sins stand higher than my head,
> they weigh on me as an unbearable weight.
> I have stinking, festering wounds,
> thanks to my folly.
> I am twisted and bent double,
> I spend my days in gloom.
>
> My loins burn with fever,
> no part of me is unscathed.
> Numbed and utterly crushed
> I groan in distress of heart.
> ....

> There is no escape for me from falling,
> no relief from my misery.
> But I make no secret of my guilt,
> I am anxious at the thought of my sin.
> ....
> Yahweh, do not desert me,
> my God, do not stand aloof from me.
> Come quickly to my help,
> Lord, my Saviour!
>
> (Psalm 38, NJB)

This understanding of illness as the result of sin can be called the theological explanation for illness.

Because illness was believed to be sent by God for the punishment or correction of sins, there was little room for the physician among the ancient Hebrews. In fact, in the Old Testament there is scarcely a reference to a physician or healer of any kind, and healing stories, such as that of the healing of Naaman by Elisha (2 Kings 5) are exceedingly rare exceptions. Moreover, when a physician is referred to, it is usually in a disparaging way. For instance, consider the story we find in 2 Chronicles. King Asa suffers from a painful disease in his feet (perhaps gout), and in his distress he consults the doctors, for which he is reprimanded by the chronicler who writes:

> In the thirty-ninth year of his reign, Asa contracted a disease in his feet, which became very severe; in his illness, however, he consulted not Yahweh but the doctors. (16:12, NJB)

Consulting a doctor was reprehensible on several counts. First, it amounted to an attempt to subvert the will of Yahweh. If Yahweh sent the illness as a correction or punishment for sin, then seeking a cure from a doctor meant nothing less than trying to avoid God's will. What is more, the doctors were almost all pagan, for no good follower of Yahweh would join a profession that tried to help people avoid God's proper chastisement.

To be sure, there were occasional departures from this extreme and rigid position about doctors. For example, in the apocryphal book of Ecclesiasticus, doctors are spoken of with more appreciation, the argument being here that God sent the illness but he also created the doctor:

> Treat the doctor with the honour that is his due,
>   in consideration of his services;
>   for he too has been created by the Lord.
> Healing itself comes from the Most High,
>   like a gift received from a king.
> The doctor's learning keeps his head high,
>   and the great regard him with awe.
> The Lord has brought forth medicinal herbs
>   from the ground,
>   and no one sensible will despise them.
>   (Ecclus. 38:1–4, NJB)

But even then we are told,

> My child, when you are ill, do not rebel,
>   but pray to the Lord and he will heal you.
> Renounce your faults, keep your hands unsoiled,
>   and cleanse your heart from all sin.
>   (vs. 9–10)

Thus, although the author of Ecclesiasticus allows room for the doctor in the healing process, he also endorses the belief that the reason for illness is sin, for which the patient must repent.

The belief in the connection between illness and sin is especially apparent in the book of Job. The whole point of the book is that Job rebels against the idea. The three "friends," Eliphaz, Bildad, and Zophar, who come to visit Job in his distress clearly regard his illness as the result of his transgressions. They do not know just what these transgressions are, but they believe they exist or Job would not be ill and would not suffer so. The illness itself, they believe, is there for the correction of Job's sins, and it is to God that Job must appeal for succor:

> Blessed are those whom God corrects!
> Do not then scorn the lesson of Shaddai!
> For he who wounds is he who soothes the sore,
> and the hand that hurts is the hand that heals.
> (Job 5:17–18, NJB. "Shaddai" is a name
> for God from the patriarchal era).

The genius of the book of Job is that Job refuses to accept the blame for his illness; he maintains steadfastly his innocence and does not agree that he deserves his suffering. He holds to this position even after Elihu comes and repeats the arguments of Job's three friends that Job must have sinned. But although Job does not agree that he deserves his suffering, he does agree that God sent the illness:

> I was living at peace, until he made me totter,
> taking me by the neck to shatter me.
> He has set me up as his target:
> he shoots his arrows at me from all sides,
> pitilessly pierces my loins,
> and pours my gall out on the ground.
> (Job 16:12–13, NJB)

As Old Testament scholar Conrad L'Heureux has pointed out, the Hebrews' belief that illness came from God made it impossible for them to develop a natural theory of illness. The natural or scientific theory of illness thus began not with the Hebrews but with the Greeks, who began the study of surgery and anatomy and realized that the heart is the center of the vascular system and that the blood carries vital elements through the body.

That the theological attitude toward illness was the prevailing belief even in Jesus' day is evidenced by the question the disciples ask him: "Rabbi, who sinned, this man or his parents, for him to have been born blind?" Not only does their question show that they still believed that disease was due to sin, it also shows that there were certain difficulties with this belief. If a person develops a disease at an advanced age, it is not hard to believe that, somewhere along the line, this person had sinned, bringing on the disease as a punishment from God. But what of a child who brought an infirmity into the world? How could a newly born child be said to have sinned? One answer might have been that the child sinned in the womb, somehow or other, hence the disciples' question implying that the man might have sinned even before he was born. The more prevalent explanation, however, was that the parents sinned and that the consequences of the parents' sin were borne by the child. In fact, we find in the Old Testament a number of examples of the belief that the consequences of a parent's sin could be borne by the child. Consider, for instance, Jeremiah 31:29 (NJB), in which the prophet quotes a proverb: "The fathers have eaten unripe grapes; the children's teeth are set on edge." Elsewhere we read that the sins of the fathers are visited upon the children to the third and fourth generations.

To be sure, this belief was repudiated by the later prophets. Jeremiah himself tells us that this saying will no longer be voiced by the people, and right after quoting the proverb, he says of it, "But each will die for his own guilt. Everyone who eats unripe grapes will have his own teeth set on edge" (v. 30, NJB). Still, old beliefs die a hard death, especially when the old beliefs support an opinion in which people have a vested interest. Those people who endorsed the theological view of illness maintained the old belief because it gave them a way to explain cases like that of the man born blind.

The important thing is that Jesus rejected this theological view of illness—at least in this instance. His reply to his disciples' question is clear: "Neither he nor his parents sinned. He was born blind so that the works of God might be displayed in him." The "works of God" in this case was the healing that Jesus wrought in the blind man. In other cases the "works of God" might be the ability of an afflicted person to live a creative and victorious life in spite of illness or disability (as Helen Keller did, for instance). For it is a fact that God's power and creativity never shine forth more clearly than when we are in the midst of affliction.

The old belief that illness was due to sin not only was still prevalent in Jesus' day, it is alive and well in our day too. Now, however, it is dressed in different clothes.

Consider the attitude taken in *The Book of Common Prayer,* 1928 edition, the official service book of the Episcopal Church until its revision in 1979. In "The Order for the Visitation of the Sick" contained in the 1928 Prayer Book, many of the prayers that the priest is supposed to use when visiting the sick state or imply that the patient's illness is due to sin. The service begins with one of the penitential psalms, which is followed by the antiphon, "Remember not, Lord, our iniquities; Nor the iniquities of our forefathers." We wonder about the inclusion of the mention of the sins of our forefathers. Perhaps the priest and penitent patient were taking no chances; just in case we *do* incur punishment for the sins of our forefathers, we had better include this petition as well as the petition for the forgiveness of our own sins, which, by implication, have to do with our illness.

This is followed by a collect, which declares: "Sanctify we beseech thee, O Lord, the sickness of this thy servant; that the sense of his weakness may add strength to his faith, and *seriousness to his repentance;* and grant that he may dwell with thee in life everlasting; through Jesus Christ our Lord."[5]

A little later in the service is a prayer to be said when the priest administers holy unction or the laying on of hands. The prayer reads: "Oh Blessed Redeemer, relieve, we beseech thee, by thy indwelling power, the distress of this thy servant; release him from sin, and drive away all pain of soul and body, that being restored to soundness of health he may offer thee praise and thanksgiving."[6] Again the implication is that the patient's illness is connected to the patient's sin.

When the Communion is said for the patient, the choice for the epistle is from Hebrews 12:5 (KJV), which reads,

> My son, despise not thou the chastening of the Lord,
> Nor faint when thou are rebuked of him:
> For whom the Lord loveth he chasteneth,
> And scourgeth every son whom he receiveth.

Again there is the idea that the illness is a chastening and rebuke by God, and for what could this chastening or rebuke be except for sin?

In fairness to the Episcopal Church, there are other portions of this office that are helpful, and in the revised Prayer Book, the Office of the Visitation of the Sick is quite a nice service. But there are other examples today of a theological view of illness; the idea of what constitutes a sin, however, is a little different. In Christian Science, for instance, the sin is "wrong thinking": if only you thought correctly, you would not be ill. The idea that this so-called wrong thinking is a sin may seem a little strong, but the basic point is that you are sick because there is something wrong with *you.*

The same idea also creeps into spiritual healing (healing through prayer, the laying on of hands, and sacramental means). Here the sin is lack of faith: If you only had sufficient faith (so the thinking goes), your prayers would be answered. No matter how charitably this point is made, the implied rebuke nevertheless remains: There is something wrong with *you;* it is *your* lack of faith.

But psychology is in the same camp. Jungian psychology, for instance, with its insistence on the importance of the individuation process for health, may say or imply that if you are ill, it means that something has gone wrong with your individuation. The antidote is, therefore, to work on your individuation process more intensely. Otherwise, the various unresolved complexes, not to mention the blocking of your psychic energy, which yearns to move toward its goal, may "somatize" itself and produce physical illness. Although this belief is not a universal tenet of Jungian psychology, it nevertheless is held by many Jungian therapists.

Of course there is truth in all of these points of view. Sometimes, as we will see in more detail shortly, illness *is* due to sin. Sometimes it is due to wrong thinking. Recovery can indeed be impeded by a lack of faith. And a failure in our psychological development may produce a psychosomatic illness, another issue we will examine more closely in a moment. But the twin dangers are that one of these factors may be regarded as the *only* cause of illness and that it may be presented in such a way that burdens the patient with feelings of guilt and lack of worth, adding to his suffering and impeding recovery.

Reincarnation

Our list of theological explanations of illness would not be complete without considering the theory of reincarnation. This theory holds that when the body dies, the soul departs from the world for a time but then returns in another body to live another life. For most believers in reincarnation, the idea of rebirth into this world is accompanied by the idea of karma—the proposition that the mode or manner of rebirth is dictated by the circumstances of our previous life. As commonly understood, karma refers to the belief that if a person has lived an unworthy life or has been guilty of certain sins or lack of fulfillment, that person will, in her next life, be born under appropriately unfavorable circumstances. Thus a believer in reincarnation and in its corollary belief, karma, would have said about the man born blind, "Yes, this man sinned, but he sinned in a former existence, and that is why he was born blind."

Such a belief is a clear example of a theological view of

illness, and the fact that many hundreds of millions of people believe in reincarnation and karma shows how deeply ingrained the theological view of illness is even today. This may also explain why, in those countries where a belief in reincarnation prevails, little is done to help the sick, for why seek to relieve illness and suffering when it is that person's karma to be ill? We might also note in passing that Jesus' answer to the disciples' question about why the man was born blind indicates that he did *not* believe in reincarnation (as some reincarnationists claim he did). Had he believed in reincarnation, the disciples' question would have provided him with exactly the right situation in which to proclaim that belief. Moreover, it would have satisfied all the moral and spiritual issues raised by the blindness of a man who had not done anything in this life to deserve it.[7]

The idea of reincarnation and karma as held by sophisticated thinkers and believers has much merit and is to be respected. In the United States, however, as one might expect, it has been popularized and loses a great deal of its subtlety and profundity. One popularization of it occurs in the idea that we "choose" everything that happens to us. If we were to ask a person of this particular religious persuasion why we were ill, he or she might answer, "Well, you know, my dear, you *chose* it." Again we have the theological view of illness, with its corollary that if you are ill, there is necessarily something wrong with *you* as a person.

For more than forty years I have functioned as a minister and psychotherapist. This work has led me to be involved with the souls of a great many people who were ill, and, of course, I myself have been ill from time to time. As a pastor and helper to these people, I have seen the damage that a misguided theological view of illness can do to the morale of the ill. When we are ill, our energy and our faith in ourselves is already diminished. We do not need a load of guilt or shame about our illness, a load that in any case may not belong to us. And should our illness clearly be the prelude to our death, a misguided understanding of what our illness means can undermine our capacity to die with courage and perhaps with serenity. For this reason, even though there is some truth in many of these theologically oriented explanations of illness, I resist the tendency to explain every illness as the result of the sins, however understood, of the suffering person. In the conflict between Job and his three friends, I'm with Job. And in the story of the healing of the man who was born blind, we have clear evidence that in Jesus' view, illness was not necessarily the result of sin.

Illness and Fate

But the questions remain. Why was this particular man singled out to be born blind? Why did he have to bear the burden of many years of blindness and misery? Why should it not have been someone else?

One answer to such questions is that it may simply have been his fate. The idea of fate is largely disregarded today, but it was of paramount importance in ancient Greece. The Greek attitude toward fate is well worth examining. The word for fate in Greek is *moira,* a word that means "lot" or "portion." Thus fate for the Greek was one's lot or portion in life, a portion that was assigned to her at the moment of her conception by three goddesses who were known as the three Moirae, or Fates. The Greeks said that at the moment of conception the first of the Fates, whose name was Clōthō, spun the thread of that person's life. A second Fate, Lachesis, measured the thread of life as it was lived out and allotted that person her share of events that she would encounter seemingly by chance, some good and some bad. The third Fate, Atropos, cut the thread of life at the fated moment and thus brought about that person's death. The Greeks had many stories about the inexorable nature of fate: Try though one might, one could not avoid one's fate. For this reason the Fates were referred to as "ye mighty Fates." In fact, so powerful were the Fates in their determination of human life that not even Zeus could alter a fate decreed by the Moirae. For this reason scholar Walter F. Otto once declared that the *real* deity of the Greeks was not Zeus but the Fates.

Not everything that happened to a person was inexorable fate, however, for in addition to *moira* there was *hypermoira*, a fate over and beyond fate. This was a fate the individual wove for herself. It was not inexorably decreed from the beginning but became a fixed fate that the individual accrued as the result of certain actions in life. The moment of death, it was believed, was always fated, but many of the events that became inevitable in a person's lifetime could have been avoided at one time.

The idea of fate is not a popular one today. In the United States, especially, we would like to believe that we can make of life what we will, that there is no divine power that inevitably shapes who we are and predetermines the moment of our death. Yet the idea of fate has its merits, for it fits certain facts of life well. It even has a certain comforting aspect, because it relieves the soul of the responsibility for certain burdens in life. It can also strengthen the soul if one adopts toward fate the Greek attitude that the real task in life was to go to meet one's fate with nobility and courage. What might constitute our fate today would include such things as the color of our skin (were we born into the world black? white? brown? red?), the kind of body we have (are we prone to fat? muscular and strong? weak and thin?), our natural intelligence (do we have a high IQ? a low IQ?), the natural amount of health we have (were we born, for instance, with congenital diabetes or Huntington's disease?), the place we were born (in the wealthy United States or impoverished Ethiopia?), and, of course, that important matter: the kind of parents to whom we were born. All of these factors are quite beyond our control and thus are part of what the Greeks would call fate.

While of great importance in ancient Greece, the idea of fate has never found a congenial home in Christianity. The early church rejected the idea because it believed it to be pagan, as did later Christian thinkers such as Thomas Aquinas, who substituted for it the rather awkward doctrine of divine providence. To be sure, there is the doctrine of predestination, which has its roots in Augustine and its flowering in Calvin. According to this doctrine, certain souls are elected to salvation and others are not. It sounds suspiciously like the old idea of fate creeping into Christianity through the back door, but theologians who believe in predestination would dispute that conclusion. Nonetheless, when the disciples asked why the man was born blind and Jesus replied that it was so God's glory might be revealed in him, something like fate or divine providence must have been in his mind.

While the word *moira* does not occur in the New Testament, one place in the writings of Paul comes close to the idea of fate. In Galatians 6:2 we read, "Bear one another's burdens, and so fulfil the law of Christ." But three verses later we read, "For each man will have to bear his own load." It's puzzling: First we are told to carry another's burdens; then we are told that each person must carry his own. The key is in the Greek words. In verse 2, the Greek word for a burden is *baros,* which means a weight or pressure (we get our English word "barometer" from it). In verse 5, the Greek word is *phortion,* which some scholars think means a load that cannot be transferred from one person to another. The word *phortion* is used to refer to the cargo of a ship, the pack carried by a solder, and the burden carried by a pregnant woman: all examples of loads that cannot readily be transferred (if at all). Now, fate is a *phortion.* It refers to all those life circumstances that no one can bear for us but that we must carry ourselves. Carrying them is like carrying the cross of Christ. Hence Jesus said, "If anyone wants to be a follower of mine, let him renounce himself and take up his cross every day and follow me" (Luke 9:23, JB. See also Matt. 16:24; Mark 8:34).

For the man born blind, blindness was the cross he had to pick up and carry. It was a kind of fate allotted to him by forces over which he had no control and no responsibility. But he was responsible for how he lived out this fate, for although we may have no control over the fixed circumstances of our lives, we do have the power to choose our attitude toward them. It can be said that our destiny evolves from the attitude we have toward our fate. Here is where the Christian idea transcends that of the ancient Greeks. For the Greeks, who believed in the inexorable nature of fate, there was no sense of a spiritual destination in life. The best one could do was to meet one's fate with nobility. "For plucking courage from despair I thought, let the worst happen, you can but meet thy fate"[8]—this is the attitude of one Greek solder who prepared himself to meet his death. For the Christian, however, life has a destiny, a spiritual destination that can be fulfilled in spite of one's fate. One could say that the Christian response to the idea of fate is not so much to deny the idea that one is born into the world with fixed circumstances but to point out that each person nonetheless has a destination that will transcend fate and lead to fulfillment.

In this way we can each transcend our fate, as it were, to reach a higher level of development. This is only possible, however, when we carry our *phortion* ourselves and stop trying to get others to carry it for us. This is spiritually like carrying our own cross: We will not blame others for our suffering but will bear our own allotted burden of pain.

The Healing of the Man by the Pool of Bethzatha

As we have already noted in our glance at the Greeks and their idea of fate, not everything that happens to us is predetermined; some things occur because of our attitudes or failures of some sort. They are *hyper-moira* in the Greek sense. In the broadest sense of the word, we can say that they may be the result of sin, and some illnesses appear to belong in this category. A good example of such an illness is found in the fifth chapter of the Gospel of John: the story of the man by the pool of Bethzatha. John tells us:

> Now there is in Jerusalem by the Sheep Gate a pool, in Hebrew called Bethzatha, which has five porticoes. In

these lay a multitude of invalids, blind, lame, paralyzed. One man was there, who had been ill for thirty-eight years. When Jesus saw him and knew that he had been lying there a long time, he said to him, "Do you want to be healed?" The sick man answered him, "Sir, I have no man to put me into the pool when the water is troubled, and while I am going another steps down before me." Jesus said to him, "Rise, take up your pallet, and walk." And at once the man was healed, and he took up his pallet and walked. (John 5:2–9)

From time to time, the waters of the pool of Bethzatha were disturbed in a mysterious way. Today we would probably explain such a phenomenon as the result of some underground disturbance, like the natural forces that cause geysers in Yellowstone National Park to erupt from time to time. Such natural explanations, however, would never have occurred to the ancients; instead they ascribed the periodic disturbances to the presence of an angel in the pool. The people believed that the first person to enter the pool after the disturbance occurred would be healed. In fact, we can well believe that some people were healed in this way—if not by an angel, then by their faith that such a healing would take place.

Now, it seemed that a certain man had been lingering by this pool for thirty-eight years and had not yet been the first one to enter the pool after the waters had been disturbed! When Jesus asks him, "Do you want to be healed?" the man avoids answering the question and makes an excuse: "Sir, I have no man to put me into the pool when the water is troubled, and while I am going another steps down before me." Was he a malingerer, someone who feigned that he wanted to be well but in fact preferred illness to health? It would seem so, not only because he has been there thirty-eight years but also because of the significance of Jesus' question. For when Jesus asks him, "Do you want to be healed?" it implies a serious doubt in Jesus' mind that the man really desired a cure. This comes out quite strongly in the Greek. The Greek word translated here as "want" (*thelō*) does not mean simply "desire" but also "will." The question really is, "Is it your willed desire to be well?"

Interestingly enough, Jesus heals the invalid even though the man does not answer his question. "Take up your pallet, and walk," Jesus commands him, and the man is cured and forced to take up his pallet and walk away, leaving the pool of the invalids behind. One would think the man might have been grateful for Jesus' cure, but he apparently resented Jesus a great deal for healing him and in fact retaliated against this man who forced him to leave his place of refuge and find a place in the world. We know of the man's attitude toward Jesus from the continuation of John's story. It seems the Pharisees discovered that the man was healed on the Sabbath. It was against the law for anyone to heal others on the Sabbath, as this constituted work, which was forbidden on the Lord's day. But when the man whom Jesus had healed learned that the authorities were on the lookout for the man who had healed him, he went to them and told them that it was Jesus who had done this outrageous thing (John 5:15). This deepened the resolve of Jesus' enemies to kill him, which was evidently part of the vengeance on Jesus that the man had hoped for.

It might seem strange that anyone would not want to be well, but there is a consequence to being well that some people want to avoid: If we are well, then we have to act and live as though we are well. This means we have to assume the burdens of work and responsibility. It is hard for many of us to believe, but some people prefer illness to health because they don't want to pay the price of health. To use Fritz Kunkel's apt expression, they are "turtles," who want to find a refuge where they can hide, or they are "clinging vines," who have persuaded themselves they can't stand on their own feet but have to have something, such as an illness, to cling to.[9] This constitutes sin, for reasons we will examine later, and this is why Jesus said to the man he healed, "See, you are well! Sin no more, that nothing worse befall you" (John 5:14).

The Greek word Jesus used here for sin is *hamartanō*. We will examine this word more closely in chapter 3 when we study the psychological meaning of the New Testament words for sin. Suffice it to say now that it means "to miss the mark" and is the same word an archer would use to indicate that his arrow had failed to hit the target. To miss the mark in life because we have kept and nourished the wrong attitudes is to sin because it thwarts God's purpose for our lives. Whereas the man born blind had to carry a certain fate, the man by the pool of Bethzatha carefully cultivated and clung to his infirmity for his egocentric purposes. It is not that his infirmity was unreal. It was real enough, and required healing, but it was the result of an impaired attitude toward life. It was what the Bible calls a sin. Psychologists would call it a psychosomatic disorder.

The power of the psyche to affect the body is great, and careful research has shown that many illnesses can be wholly or partly attributed to psychic disturbances. For instance, in his book *The Broken Heart*, James Lynch has demonstrated that the incidence of heart disease increases significantly when people are lonely and emotionally isolated. Both psychological disorders and spiritual disorders can produce illness or open us up to illness by weakening the body's defenses. No one knows how many illnesses are wholly or partly psychologically induced, but such instances abound.

Yet we can take this truth too far. I recall a point in my life when I was so impressed by the truths of psychosomatic medicine that I began to see all illness as the result of psychological or spiritual malfunction. But I also recall what a doctor friend once said to me when I was expounding to him my ideas of psychosomatic illness. "That is all well and good," said my friend, "but never forget that everything that is alive is under constant attack."[10]

Of course that is true. Our bodies are under constant attack. Frequently, perhaps even continuously, our immune system destroys viruses, bacteria, and cancer cells so quickly and so efficiently that we are unaware of the biochemical warfare being waged within us. If it were not for our body's toughness and resourcefulness, those infinitesimal attackers would quickly overwhelm us, as people discover when they have immune-system disorders such as AIDS. Moreover, it is not only human beings who are attacked by illnesses but animals and plants as well. If our dog succumbs to cancer, is it necessarily psychosomatic? If our rose bush is weakened by rust or black spot disease, should we call the psychiatrist? Do plants and animals become ill because they sin?

The Greek playwright Aeschylus perceived the truth that illness and health are never far from each other. He wrote, "Of a truth, lusty health rests not content within its due bounds; for disease ever presses close against it, its neighbor with a common wall."[11]

It seems clear that Jesus regarded some illnesses as the

result of sin. Consider what Jesus says to the paralytic in Luke 5:20: "Man, your sins are forgiven you." And when the Pharisees challenged him for daring to forgive sins, Jesus says, "Which is easier, to say, 'Your sins are forgiven you,' or to say, 'Rise and walk'?" (Luke 5:23).

Not all cases of illness in the Gospels were seen as the result of sin, however. In certain cases, as we will now see, illness could actually be an integral part of a person's individuation process.

Illness as Part of our Journey to Wholeness

In the introduction, we talked about the individuation process. We described it as a process, initiated from the unconscious, that seeks to bring us to a state of wholeness. This process is always difficult to describe because it is accomplished differently by each person. My path is not your path, and your path is not anyone else's. As a psychotherapist, I work with my clients to try to discover where their path lies, but we have to discover the path together, sniffing out the way, as it were, like two hounds on the track of their quarry. In our present culture we extoll the merits of health, and most of us seek to live healthy lives, dreading and shunning illness if we can. However, sometimes it seems that illness plays its own peculiar role in our path to wholeness. The writers of the Bible understood this truth; Luke gives us a good example in the story of the healing of the woman with the issue of blood. Luke tells the story as follows:

> As he [Jesus] went, the people pressed round him. And a woman who had had a flow of blood for twelve years and

could not be healed by any one, came up behind him, and touched the fringe of his garment; and immediately her flow of blood ceased. And Jesus said, "Who was it that touched me?" When all denied it, Peter said, "Master, the multitudes surround you and press upon you!" But Jesus said, "Some one touched me; for I perceive that power has gone forth from me." And when the woman saw that she was not hidden, she came trembling, and falling down before him declared in the presence of all the people why she had touched him, and how she had been immediately healed. And he said to her, "Daughter, your faith has made you well; go in peace." (Luke 8:42–48)

We will look at one intriguing detail and make three major points about this story. The detail involves the comparison of this story as we find it in Luke to the way we find it in Mark. The two stories are identical except for a comment in Mark not found in Luke. Mark says, "Now there was a woman who had suffered from a haemorrhage for twelve years; after long and painful treatment under various doctors, she had spent all she had without being any the better for it, in fact, she was getting worse" (5:25–26, JB). Luke omits the part about the unsuccessful and expensive treatment by the doctors. It is pretty well accepted by scholars that Luke transposed most of Mark's Gospel into his own, adding his own material to it. If this is so, why did Luke omit the verse about the doctors? No doubt it is because Luke himself was a physician and did not like the aspersions it cast upon his profession! The omission is an interesting human touch in the excellent Gospel of Luke. The three points that we will now examine, however, have somewhat broader ramifications for our culture today.

The first point concerns the statement that Jesus makes

in Mark 5:30. When the woman touches Jesus' garment, he asks, "Who touched my garments?" Everyone denies it, and the disciples point out that there is a crowd of people pressing close to Jesus; they don't understand why Jesus should ask who touched him. But Jesus knows someone has touched him in a special way because he felt that power had gone out of him. The Greek word translated "power" might just as well have been translated "energy." The fact that Jesus knows power or energy went out of him at the woman's touch tells us that the work of the healer requires an expenditure of energy. This is particularly true when the healing is accomplished through the interaction of the personalities of the healer and the person being healed. This is the case with psychotherapy and with spiritual healing. It is the reason that this kind of work is exhausting and that people can do only so much of it. As someone once put it, doing the work of psychological or spiritual healing is like giving people a blood transfusion—you have only so much to give.

People in healing professions that call for such close interaction with patients have the special problem of finding appropriate ways to replenish the psychic energy that goes out of them in the course of their work. Not only psychotherapists but many other people find that their work depletes them of energy—not just physical energy, but psychic energy. To lose psychic energy is to feel a deep-down tiredness. To maintain their effectiveness and the health and vigor of soul and body, such people must find ways of replenishing the lost energy. Certain techniques, prayer included, may not help, because many ways of finding energy require a certain amount of psychic energy to start with.

For this reason, many people whose work or life exhausts their supply of psychic energy may need to turn to the body to find their renewal. People with an athletic inclination (it doesn't have to be much) may find that exercising at the end of the day "cleans them out" and gets them back inside themselves. This exercise might be jogging, swimming, or walking at a pace rapid enough to get heart and lungs working, or playing sports such as soccer or tennis. What exercise we utilize will depend to a large extent on our physical body type. Those among us who are the lean, hungry type may find jogging satisfying; others with a heavier body build may turn to swimming or walking.

During exercise, the body purifies itself through the process of sweating. The deep breathing necessitated by moderate-to-vigorous exercise not only further cleanses the body but also tends to relieve depression. Minds overtaxed by ingesting too much of the psyche of other people can now find a way back into themselves. The fantasies that accompany all repetitive exercise, such swimming long distances or jogging, liberate the soul to find its own natural, restoring activity.

For people for whom rigorous exercise may not be the answer, gardening may be a good alternative. Merely being with plants is healing to the soul, and tending to them cares not only for the plants but also for that in us which grows. It is a curious but fascinating fact that in the Greek language the word for healing (*therapeuō*) means not only to heal but also to render service to the gods and to cultivate a garden! Perhaps it is Mother Earth who heals us even as we work closely with her. For others, hatha yoga may help. Hatha yoga comes from India, but the practice of this kind of yoga does not require espousing a foreign spiritual belief system, because it is based entirely upon certain meditative exercises developed in concert with bodily movements.

To return to our story about the woman with the issue of blood, the second point to be noted is that although the woman had been ill for twelve years and had sought cures from many different people with no success, she had persevered in her search for health. Unlike the man by the pool of Bethzatha, she did not sit by the side of the road finding an excuse for her illness but went actively in search of a cure. Clearly she was no malingerer and her illness was not psychosomatic. Eventually she found her healing through Jesus. A point is made in this story: If she had been cured earlier by one of the many physicians Mark tells us she had consulted, she would not have been led to seek out and find Jesus. *Thus her illness was the driving factor that kept her searching until she found him.* Had she been healed earlier she would not have been led to him.

What difference does it make whether she was healed by Jesus or by someone else? Doesn't it all add up to the same thing in the end? It does make a difference, and the story as we find it in both Mark and Luke brings this difference out clearly by the choice of the Greek word they use to denote the kind of healing Jesus performed for her.

Jesus tells the woman, "Daughter, your faith has made you well; go in peace." Unfortunately, the English does not do justice to the meaning of the Greek. In the Greek language there are many words for healing; almost all of them occur in the New Testament in one place or another. One of them, *therapeuō*, we have already discussed. It is the word from which we derive our English words "therapy" and "therapist." It can be found in Matthew 4:23, 24; 8:16; and in Luke 7:21; 8:2; 9:1; and 10:9. In the Greek mind the activities of healing, rendering service to the worship of the divine, and cultivating the land were all related activities. Healing is ultimately a religious enterprise, for to become well and remain well means serving those powers inside ourselves that essentially constitute the God within. The soul herself is like a garden: Neglected, she goes to seed and brings forth weeds, becoming weak and drying up for lack of attention. It was Socrates who first spoke of the need for a "care of the soul," and this concern for the soul has come down into Christianity which, at least in times past, had its own methods for caring for the soul, though nowadays these methods are often sadly neglected. In those forms of psychotherapy that pay heed to the soul and the inner life, the therapy always includes a certain caring or tending of the soul, methods we will look at in more detail later on.

Several other Greek words for healing deserve our attention here. The first is *iaomai,* and its noun counterpart *iatros,* which is the Greek word for a physician. *Iaomai* is the word used in Mark 5:26 in reference to the woman's unsuccessful search for a cure for her hemorrhage. Other examples of its usage occur in Matthew 13:15; Luke 7:7; 8:48; 9:2, 11; 14:4; 1 Corinthians 12:9, 28, 30; and Hebrews 12:13. This word also means to heal or cure, but without the overtones of meaning that we find in *therapeuō.* The word *iatros* has recently found a place in English in the relatively new word "iatrogenic." This word is compounded from the word *iatros* (physician) and the word *genesis* (beginning or origination). An iatrogenic disease is therefore a disease the doctor caused. Fortunately, the overwhelming number of doctors are skillful people who are most helpful in the cure of disease, but given the complexity of modern medicine and the side effects of powerful drugs, now and then something is bound to go wrong, bringing on an iatrogenic disease.

Another important Greek word is *hygiainō,* which means to be in sound health. The adjectival form is *hygiēs,* which means hale, sound in health. Our English word "hygiene" comes from the same root, and one of the daughters of Asclepius, Greek god of healing, is named Hygieia.

Thus, there are a number of words Jesus could have used when he told the woman she had been healed, but the word he chose was not, strictly speaking, a medical term at all but a spiritual and religious word: *sōzō.*[12] This word, which is usually rendered in English translations by expressions such as "you have been made well," means to save, to rescue, to preserve from being lost, to deliver or to set free. Thus while the lesser Greek words for healing refer to cures and the restoration of physical or mental health, *sōzō* denotes the restoration of a person to a state of wholeness in every way, spiritual as well as physical. It denotes not only healing but salvation.

There is a distinct pattern to Jesus' use of the word *sōzō* and his use of lesser words for healing. In every instance when the person who was healed did not make an extended effort to find healing, Jesus used a lesser Greek word to denote the cure. An example is the healing of the centurion's servant (Matt. 8:5–13). In this story the ill servant does not come himself to Jesus but is healed at the behest of the centurion. Jesus, beholding the faith of the centurion, says to him, "Go back, then; you have believed, so let this be done for you" (v. 13, JB). Matthew then tells us, "And the servant was cured at that moment" (v. 13, JB). The word here used for "cured" is not *sōzō* but *iaomai.* In the New Testament, only when a person is active in pursuing her own healing, putting herself on the line, so to speak, does that person find that total restoration denoted in the New Testament by the word *sōzō*.

Psychotherapists know the importance of the effort put forth by the client if the psychotherapeutic process is to succeed. If a client is passive, waiting and expecting someone else to heal him, the possibilities for healing are greatly limited. In psychotherapy the therapist and the client work together on the healing process or it does not succeed. Purely physical conditions, of course, can often be cured by a doctor through the use of drugs or surgery even though the patient is relatively passive in the healing process. But even here the healing process is greatly aided if the patient participates in some way. Today many healing practitioners use methods of meditation with their patients, guiding them through appropriate imagery in a healing process. Such meditative aids enlist the help of the patient's imagination and quite often also enlist the help of the patient's faith. It was my mother who pioneered this work of combining active forms of meditation with prayer in order to facilitate healing; many others have now taken up the technique, using it in their own way.

Now we see our third point, the paradoxical nature of the story of the healing of the hemorrhaging woman: Her illness was an essential step on her way to wholeness. As mentioned earlier, if she had been cured by well-intentioned doctors, she would have overcome her malady, but she would not have been changed and renovated in soul and spirit as well as in body. Sometimes, it seems, an illness serves the purposes of individuation, keeping us on the path for healing until we have found the way we are to go. The story of the woman who touched Jesus' garment has always been of special importance to me since my own illness, which I described in the prologue, was not curable by the many well-intentioned and well-trained people to whom I went for a cure. I was forced, as a consequence, to keep searching until my search led to Kunkel, who helped me find a healing that not only relieved my anxiety but changed my whole life.

We are now in a position to draw certain conclusions about illness and healing as seen from the perspective of the Gospels. The healing stories we have considered show us that illness may come for several different reasons and have a variety of meanings. In some cases, sin, taken in its broadest sense, may be a major factor in producing the illness. In other cases the illness may be simply an act of fate: We may be born with it, or born with a predisposition to it, or become the victim of some epidemic. Finally, there are certain illnesses of body or soul that might be brought upon us to impel us to find the path to our individuation. These illnesses have a way of continuing until we find that path to healing that will lead us into a greatly expanded life and consciousness. In such cases the illness is an integral part of our journey to wholeness.

Because of the variety of possible causes of illness, it is best to approach each case of illness with an open mind and not prejudge its causes. If we ourselves are ill, we need to examine the meaning and causes of our illness from many angles. If we are healers, it is best to let the individual meaning of each illness gradually become clear and not impose on the ill person a preconceived idea or prejudice of our own. Especially in cases of psychological disorders, or physical disorders with a strong psychological concomitant, it is best to wait patiently for the meaning of the illness gradually to become clear, for to "know" its meaning in advance would be to become blind to the true message the illness is trying to send.

Such was certainly the case with the woman with the issue of blood. Driven by her need and led by her faith, she found her way to the source of healing herself. So to her Jesus said, "Daughter, your faith has made you well." But just what is this thing called faith? It is to this that we now turn.

2

....

Faith and Knowledge
in the Healing Process

Faith and knowledge are both vital to healing. But they
are very different categories, and their relationship has
long been misunderstood in the field of psychotherapy. In
this chapter we will examine that relationship and explore
the roles of faith and knowledge in the healing process.

Knowledge

Modern psychotherapy, from its inception with Sigmund
Freud, has placed a great emphasis on the importance of
knowing. Freud believed that if we analyzed those unconscious psychological processes that had hitherto been
dominating our psychic life, we would acquire a knowledge about ourselves that would be instrumental in our
healing. The method by which this knowledge was acquired he called psychoanalysis.

Carl Jung, Freud's younger contemporary in the early

explorations of the unconscious, disagreed with Freud on certain issues but agreed with him on the importance of self-knowledge for psychological healing. For Freud, this knowledge concerned the analysis of those personal historical, developmental factors, mostly from childhood, that he believed were the contents of the unconscious. For Jung, knowledge of the personal unconscious was also important, but he further believed that a knowledge of the collective unconscious was essential if a complete healing and redirection of life were to take place. This collective unconscious, as we have already noted in the introduction, includes patterns and structures of the human psyche, found universally, which Jung called the archetypes. It also included the Self or psychic Center, which, as we have seen, seeks to draw a person into inner development aimed at wholeness. For this latter process to succeed, the participation of consciousness is essential. Unless one knows oneself, individuation cannot take place. For Jung, crucial to therapeutic success was the self-knowledge that came from knowing not only one's personal psyche but also the effects of the archetypes on us and the direction in which the individuation process was seeking to move us.

Thus, for both Freud and Jung, "analysis" came to be virtually synonymous with "knowledge of oneself." This is suggested by the root meaning of the word "analysis," which comes from the Greek *analysis,* which means "to loose or dissolve" and refers to any activity in which a whole is broken down into its component parts so the latter can be more closely examined. The knowledge gained from this analysis enables the ego to stand apart from unconscious influences and to no longer be swallowed or unconsciously driven by them. Unconscious personal complexes are no longer so destructive once they are understood, and archetypal patterns that could slavishly dominate the personality can be put to creative use once we become aware of them. Perhaps only those who have experienced a successful analysis can know how freeing it is to be able to say, "Oh, I see now what it is that has been driving me so!" Things are different now solely because we *know*.

Interestingly enough, the unconscious itself seems to want to be known. It is as though the various parts of our unconscious personality want to share in the light of consciousness. In fact, a great sin of the ego (as we will examine more closely in chapter 3) is not to know. In the dreams of people in analysis, a common motif is that the client comes for the analytical session only to discover that other, unknown people are also there to see the analyst. Usually the dreamer is disturbed by this and can't understand why the analyst puts up with the intrusion of these strangers. One meaning of such a dream is that it describes aptly the interest the various aspects of the unconscious are taking in what is going on in the analysis. They want to share in it, to be known and to know themselves. It seems that the ego is not the only part of the Self concerned with process of knowledge.

What is more, the collective unconscious is itself a great repository of knowledge. It is as though everything the human race ever knew continues to exist in the collective unconscious. This is sometimes represented by dreams in which a great library appears. For Jung himself, it was the ancient lore of alchemy that caught his attention. The lore of alchemy, in modern times almost entirely forgotten, contained for Jung an invaluable storehouse of symbolism regarding the way wholeness emerges in human personality.

The knowledge contained in the collective unconscious also seems to contain an intimation of knowledge not yet known on a conscious level but within the possibility of becoming known. For instance, new scientific ideas have a way of emerging into the consciousness of many people almost simultaneously, and one can trace the seeds of these new ideas back through history. The idea of evolution, for instance, has a long history and emerged simultaneously in the minds of Charles Darwin and of his friend and associate, Alfred Russel Wallace. The idea of the unconscious itself, as L. L. Whyte has shown, had a long history of development before Freud and had occurred to Jung independently of Freud at about the same time.[1]

For good reasons, therefore, Jung was greatly impressed with the importance of knowledge in the healing process. With his classical bent of mind, he looked for antecedents to his depth psychology and thought he found them in Gnosticism. Gnosticism was a movement prevalent in the second and third centuries A.D. that emphasized the importance for salvation of acquiring a saving knowledge. It is from *gnōsis,* a Greek word for knowledge, that the word "Gnosticism" is derived. For the Gnostics, the souls of those persons who contained within themselves sparks of the divine light and who acquired the saving knowledge of their true heavenly origins could be saved. Because of their knowledge, at death they could pass on to reunion with the spiritual "pleroma," or fullness of God above, and not have to be reborn into the material world of ignorance and darkness. For reasons that go beyond the scope of this work to explore, the Gnostics believed that only they possessed the necessary knowledge of our true origins with the God above. Believing as they did in the saving powers of this metaphysical knowledge, they disparaged faith, especially the seemingly simple faith of the Christians, with whom they were often in competition.

Jung shared with the Gnostics their belief that knowledge saves. Later, when he discovered the rich psychological symbolism of alchemy, he came to believe that the alchemists were the successors of the Gnostics in looking to inner experience for a source of knowledge. He once wrote, "Now for the Gnostics—and this is their real secret—the psyche existed as a source of knowledge just as much as it did for the alchemists."[2]

One would think that, with the discovery of the saving efficacy of psychological knowledge, depth psychology would have developed a certain optimism or hopefulness about life and the human situation. However, the fact is that some of the early promise of depth psychology has not been fulfilled. Freud believed that, even with all the knowledge of oneself gained through psychoanalysis, the best that could be hoped for was a kind of standoff in which the ego, armed with its self-knowledge about the dangerous urges of the unconscious, could better manage its life. But there was no salvation in it, no release from an essential pessimism, because Freud discovered no God in the depths of the unconscious, nor any workings of a divine power. Basically Freud believed it was up to the unaided human ego to work things out as best it could, and at the end of life, there was nothing. This is what Freud saw; this is what he believed, and he must be given credit for being an honest thinker.

Things might have turned out differently with the depth psychology of Jung, for as we have seen, Jung discovered in the unconscious the workings of the individuation process, which points toward a goal, a certain life fulfillment, and therefore seems to endow life with a sense of purpose and meaning. We cannot say that Jung viewed life as benign, for no one saw more clearly than Jung the dark nature of the powers at work in the human psyche. Nevertheless, the mere fact that, in spite of the evil at work in our lives, a purpose also seemed to exist, might have led Jung to at least a cautious optimism about the ultimate meaning of life. In fact, at times Jung did seem to have the cautiously hopeful attitude that there must be an ultimate destiny for the human soul that is real and worth striving for.

But at other times Jung came up with a pessimism as profound as that of Freud because it was his belief that the Self was as much evil as it was good. In his book *Answer to Job,* Jung reaches the pessimistic conclusion that the fundamental agency of human evil is the psychic Center itself and that this Center strives as much for evil as it does for good. Since the Center or Self is the *imago dei* in the soul, it is like saying that God is the author of evil and good equally. Furthermore, in *Answer to Job,* Jung said that only the ego possesses consciousness and that this God within us is blind, unconscious, and morally undifferentiated.

Perhaps it was because of Jung's belief that the God within us is equally good and evil that he found little room in his outlook for faith. As we will note, he disparaged faith especially in relationship to knowledge.

Faith

In contrast to knowledge, psychology disregards or disparages faith. The word "faith" rarely occurs in psychological literature, it will not be found, for instance, in any dictionaries of psychology. Psychotherapists in their training hardly ever hear faith discussed. Whereas knowledge is a reputable scientific word and category, faith has the aura of something unscientific, blind, and perhaps even foolish.

Jung himself seldom discussed faith, but when he did mention it, it was usually, though not always, in a hostile and depreciatory fashion. A few quotations from Jung will make this clear. Consider, for instance, his contrast between faith and knowledge:

> Modern man abhors faith and the religions based upon it. He holds them valid only so far as their knowledge-content seems to accord with his own experience of the psychic background. He wants to *know*—to experience for himself.[3]

Faith and knowledge for Jung were so far apart that he believed they were separated by a virtually impassable chasm:

> [A] gulf has opened out between *faith* and *knowledge.* The contrast has become so enormous that one is obliged to speak of the incommensurability of these two categories and their way of looking at the world.[4]

Not only are faith and knowledge separated by a wide gulf, faith, in fact, was inimical to knowledge in Jung's eyes:

> For just as knowledge is not faith, so faith is not knowledge. We are concerned here with things that can be disputed, that is, with knowledge, but not with indisputable faith, which precludes critical discussion at the outset. The oft-repeated paradox "knowledge through faith" seeks in vain to bridge the gulf that separates the two.[5]

As an enemy to knowledge, faith, in Jung's view, is also an enemy to maturity and growth. He said of faith that it

tries to retain a primitive mental condition on merely sentimental grounds. It is unwilling to give up the primitive, childlike relationship to mind-created and hypostatized figures; it wants to go on enjoying the security and confidence of a world still presided over by powerful, responsible, and kindly parents. Faith may include a *sacrificium intellectus* (provided there is an intellect to sacrifice), but certainly not a sacrifice of feeling. In this way the faithful *remain* children instead of becoming *as* children, and they do not gain their life because they have not lost it. Furthermore, faith collides with science and thus gets its deserts, for it refuses to share in the spiritual adventure of our age.[6]

Jung's rejection of faith began early in his life. In his autobiography, *Memories, Dreams, Reflections,* he tells how he eagerly awaited his confirmation when his father, a clergyman, would explain to him the doctrine of the Trinity, in which, though only a boy, he had become quite intrigued. But when the time came for the great explanation of this mystery, his father dismissed the whole subject with the mere statement that one could not understand it but simply had to believe it on faith. That finished off Jung with faith, for as far as he was concerned there was no point in going around believing in things that could not be known. It also lowered his father in his eyes and laid the foundation for his departure from the church, for he came to see the church as a place for the dead, not for the living. Since the church apparently had forsaken the way of knowledge and clung instead to blind faith, how could it do otherwise than spiritually die?

Much of Jung's position about faith rings true. Some

people do seem to cling to "blind faith" as a way to escape a mature facing of doubts. Often people do refuse to find out the truth lest it damage their so-called faith. Faith does indeed seem to collide with science, and the truth is often sacrificed for the sake of protecting a cherished belief system. Yet a category that has been around for as long as faith must surely have something positive going for it. After all, Jesus himself declared to the woman with the issue of blood that it was her faith that saved her. The writers of the New Testament, who were neither fools nor immature children, had a great deal to say in favor of it; indeed, some of those early Christians were even willing to die for something that they called their faith. So faith deserves a hearing; a word needs to be spoken in its defense, and I propose to undertake such a defense, resting it on one major thesis: that faith, properly regarded and as understood in the New Testament, is not, as Jung supposed, a category of the intellect but a *category of the soul*. When this difference is understood, faith can be seen in an entirely different light, its importance for healing can be understood, and its apparent opposition to knowledge will no longer exist.

As a category of the intellect, faith amounts to a willingness to assent and cling to beliefs even though they cannot be validated by any kind of proof. Faith as a category of the soul can be thought of as that investment of energy by the soul in pursuit of what the soul finds to be meaningful. While faith as an intellectual category seizes upon supposed certainties, faith as a category of the soul impels the soul to search for the sources of spiritual life and sustains the soul in this search. The mind can be said to flourish with knowledge and the soul to live and grow with both knowledge and faith. For faith is the sustenance of the soul as food is of the body, and without some faith the soul weakens and dies.

Faith could also be said to be closer to feeling than to thinking. Jung himself said as much, but he said it in a way that seemed to disparage feeling: "Faith may include a *sacrificium intellectus* . . . , but certainly not a sacrifice of feeling." Now, feeling is as important as thinking. If a person does not think, that person's mind is dead; if a person does not feel, that person's soul is dead.

Perhaps the richest source of knowledge we have about the faith of the soul is the New Testament, and if we look at the New Testament it becomes apparent at once that while Jesus cared a great deal about faith and the soul, he showed a surprising lack of interest in anyone's belief system, except insofar as it affected a person's soul. He almost never asked a person theological questions or wanted to know if anyone believed the "right things" about God, and he showed a surprising lack of interest in what we would call religious doctrine. He was concerned about the religious belief system of the Pharisees only because it led them into what he saw as hypocrisy and other sins of the soul. What did concern him was what lay within a person's heart, for this showed him what was happening in the soul, and it was the soul that was of paramount importance.

Insight into the nature of this faith by which the soul lives is aided by the Greek words used in the New Testament for faith. The noun is *pistis,* which is related to and stems from the Greek verb *peithō,* which means "to persuade." If the soul has faith, then the soul can be said to be persuaded of something or persuaded by someone. That which persuades the soul, however, is seldom rational in nature. To love someone, for instance, is to be persuaded in the soul about that person. Knowledge proceeds by what it knows, but when the soul is persuaded, it enables us to follow a certain course of action even when we have no way of knowing for certain what its outcome will be. To paraphrase Pascal, the heart has its reasons the mind knows not of.

In English we speak of having faith, but in the New Testament such an expression seldom occurs. Instead the verb for "having faith," *pisteuō,* when used transitively, requires a preposition (*en, eis,* or *epi*) to complete its meaning. Thus we do not "have faith"; we put our faith *into* someone or something.[7] This means that faith must have a place in which to be invested for it to live and grow, a point upon which we will further comment shortly.

This faith of which the New Testament speaks is not arrived at by an act of will. We cannot manufacture faith by just deciding to have it. Something must be the source of our faith as well as its object. This is apparent in a peculiar grammatical construction in Greek known as the object genitive. For the nonreader of Greek, this may seem like a fine point to pursue, but it will lead to a deepening insight into the New Testament meaning of faith. In the Greek language, nouns have different cases: nominative, genitive, dative, accusative, and vocative. When it comes to an expression such as "it is faith in that name [of Jesus] that has restored this man to health, as you can all see" (Acts 3:16*b*) the word *pistis* (faith) stands in the dative case to denote that faith was the agent of transformation, and the Greek for "his *name*" stands in the genitive case. Ordinarily we might suppose "name" would be in the accusative case since it appears to be the object of the man's faith. But in the thinking of the New Testament, that which is the *object* of the faith is also the *source* of the faith, and the use of the genitive case expresses this nuance of meaning. Thus when the New Testament speaks of "faith in Christ" it means that the faith that we put into Christ is also originated by Christ. Similarly, when the New Testament speaks about the love of God, it puts "love" in the nominative case and "God" in the genitive case. This means that our love for God is originated by God, for God is not only its object but also its source.

This takes us back to the story of the woman with the issue of blood. We will recall that in this story Jesus said to her, "Daughter, your faith has made you well; go in peace." It is clear that this woman's faith had nothing to do with creeds or with her theological beliefs. Jesus never asked her about such things. Rather, the faith Jesus commended was a category of the soul; it was an urge from her soul toward Jesus, who was both the object of her faith and the source of it. It was this that led to her complete healing and renewal. It was because of this faith that she kept persevering until she was led to Jesus, and it was this faith that led to her complete healing and renewal.

Faith in the Healing Relationship

In the language of psychotherapy we would call the relationship between the woman and Jesus the "transference." "Transference" is the word used in psychotherapy for the energy and expectations the client brings into the therapeutic relationship. Transference is regarded as a very important part of psychotherapy. Freud made a great deal of it; in Jungian work, too, as well as in other psychotherapies, it is widely regarded as the most important part of the process of healing. Consequently, the transference has been analyzed and discussed at great length. The client, for instance, may project into the therapist the mother image or the father image and may reexperience with the therapist all kinds of childhood traumas. The therapist may also carry for the client the projections of the savior, the positive parent, the negative parent, or even the lover. Because of its importance, innumerable articles and books have been written about the psychology of the transference, but to the best of my knowledge no one has pointed out its most important element: faith.

Faith as such is not identical with the transference, but faith is its essential ingredient. If the process of psychotherapy is to succeed, the client must bring into the relationship with the therapist an element of faith. Part of the work of the therapist is to hold the faith of the client for him. If this faith is not present, the work will not succeed; in fact, it is highly unlikely that it will have started in the first place. The faith that a client brings into a relationship with a therapist may be very small at first. It may be only a tiny seed, almost invisible and clouded over by depression or despair. Nevertheless, it supplies the energy for persevering in the hard psychological work that must be done. Faith, like the mustard seed in the New Testament parable, can be a seemingly insignificant thing from which great work develops.

Since the therapist is the receptacle for the faith without which the healing process will not even begin, much less succeed, the therapist must be conscientious in her work, diligent in working on her own soul, and, by virtue of her integrity, worthy of being the temporary carrier of this faith. She must know enough about herself and her shadow, her dark side, that she does not take advantage of the transference in any way that would prove inimical to the healing of the client. She must strive to understand the nature of this transference and be conscious enough of herself and her own foibles that her blind spots do not destroy that faith.

For these reasons the most important element in the healing relationship is the personality, knowledge, and integrity of the healer. No amount of book knowledge, no skill in using therapeutic techniques, and no academic degrees, no matter how prestigious, can rival in importance the wholeness of the personality of the therapist. As Jung himself once put it, the healer *is* the healing. What is more, the healer must know that while she is temporarily the receptacle of the client's faith, the ultimate success of the work depends on the eventual realization by the client that the healing is in himself. This realization will be greatly aided if the therapist also understands that all healing comes from God—or from the *imago dei* in the psyche that Jung called the Self.

The therapist, like the client, needs to have faith in the healing process, for sometimes it is only the faith of the therapist that sustains the work of healing when the going gets tough. This kind of faith is not something one can acquire by going to school; it can only come to the therapist from her own experience. The most important experience a therapist can have for the nourishment of her faith in the healing process is her own cure. Many therapists, for this reason, emerge from the ranks of those who were themselves once deeply troubled and managed to find a way to health again. While such an experience is not necessarily the only way to arrive at the faith a therapist needs in order to be a healer, it is probably the most efficacious way. For this reason we speak of the wounded healer, the healer who herself was once damaged and, through the ministration given to her own wounds and the healing of them, has acquired faith in the powers of healing.

For this reason, those therapeutic measures the therapist can employ most successfully with her client will largely be those measures that healed her. Therein lies her power, for this method of healing she knows from her soul, not simply from her intellect. This means we need different kinds of therapists, who have found their healing in different ways, so that human need can be met completely. For the same reason, if the therapist realizes that her particular approach to healing is not going to be efficacious with a particular client, she must be ready and willing to refer the client to another therapist whose different experience may be more helpful than hers in this particular case.

Because the faith of the therapist that sustains the work lies in her trust that within the client's psyche are the powers that will heal him, she will also know that the ultimate faith of the client must find its object not in her as the therapist but in those powers within himself that guide and heal him. When this happens, the client no longer needs the therapist, or at least does not need the therapist in the way he did at first. The nature of the transference then changes, or even dissolves entirely, as the original relationship between the client and therapist is changed by the client's growing realization that he has a source of healing within himself from which wholeness emerges. This change in the client-therapist relationship may be smooth and amicable, or it may be stormy as the client breaks free from dependence on the therapist in ways that may resemble an adolescent breaking away from his parents. However it takes place, the therapist must be wise enough to understand what is happening and accept the change. She also must be sufficiently free of her own ego-centric needs that she does not unconsciously try to keep the client from moving on.

Faith in Medical Healing

Although the transference is especially important in the psychotherapeutic relationship, it is also important in medical healing. The healing process is aided by the patient's faith in the medical doctor. The doctor may carry for the ill person the projection of the healer and savior, and this may work advantageously for the healing process by arousing in the patient positive emotions and a hopeful outlook. A wise physician knows this and provides opportunities in her relationship with the patient for a certain amount of personal interaction; she does not reduce the relationship to a purely technical one. However, since the healing used by the doctor involves more or less mechanical or methodical procedures, such as surgery and drugs, which would have a certain efficacy regardless of whether the patient has faith in the doctor, the transference is generally of less significance in medical practice than in psychotherapeutic practice.

Idolatrous Faith Versus Faith in God

The need of the soul for faith and for a receptacle in which to place that faith is great. If there is no suitable receptacle in which that faith can be placed, it may then be placed in an unsuitable one. Misguided or malevolent political leaders may be the recipients of this faith, and a good deal of deviltry may result. Fritz Kunkel has shown that the Self may be projected into seemingly charismatic leaders who have an instinct for gathering the faith of their followers and using the resultant power for demonic purposes. He calls this "psychological feudalism" and regards it as a form of idolatry.[8] Because it is a collective movement in which individual consciousness is not only discouraged but repressed, the evil and darkness that result can be phenomenal. Hitler's Germany is the outstanding example in this century. Horrible though such episodes in history are, they bear testimony to the need of the soul for faith and for a suitable place in which to put it.

With the increasing consciousness of the client and the gradual resolution of the transference, the client can begin to have a relationship with her own Center, no longer projecting the Center into the therapist. The nourisher of that person's faith is then her own inner process which emanates from her creative Center. Religiously speaking, it amounts to faith in a God within. No longer does the client look outside of herself for the power that heals and saves, making idols of people or movements; instead she finds it within herself. Jesus said the kingdom of God is not coming with signs to be observed; "neither shall they say, Lo here! or, lo there! for, behold, the kingdom of God is within you" (Luke 17:21, KJV).[9]

Care of the Soul

With a growing appreciation of the fact that healing for our souls originates within ourselves, just as does the healing of the body, comes an awareness of the importance of caring for that inner being we call the soul. The first person to speak of the need to care for the soul may have been Socrates. When he was charged by the Athenian authorities with the crime of perverting the youth of Athens, his answer was that he never did so but only taught people about the need for the care of the soul. So Socrates declared to one of his detractors,

> Most excellent man, are you who are a citizen of Athens, the greatest of cities and the most famous for its wisdom and power, not ashamed to care for the acquisition of wealth and for reputation and honor, when you neither care nor take thought for wisdom and truth and the perfection of your soul? . . . For I go about doing nothing else than urging you, young and old, not to care for your persons or your property more than for the perfection of your souls.[10]

Socrates' belief can be compared to statements made by Jesus about the soul, such as this one in Matthew 16:26 (KJV): "For what is a man profited, if he shall gain the whole world, and lose his own soul? or what shall a man give in exchange for his soul?"

When Socrates made his statement, it was such a radical idea that he was condemned to die for it. From Socrates the idea of the care of the soul found its way into early Christianity, the idea being that the soul was corruptible and perishable, but with care it could become incorruptible and imperishable thanks to the presence of Christ within it. Today the idea of the care of the soul has fallen on hard times except for the survival of certain mystical and introspective forms of Christianity and certain other religions, and for its reappearance in certain psychologies, especially in Jungian psychology. In Jungian psychology much of the healing method involves keeping a journal, recording dreams, and doing active imagination, creative writing, painting, and sculpting, all of which are forms of the care of the soul. In this way the soul can remain healthy, as a garden stays healthy when it is cared for, and its faith is nurtured and directed to the creative Center, which is its true source of strength and healing. Contemporary Christianity, while not entirely turning its back on the soul, has been largely without a method of healing for the soul. Fortunately, most of the methods of caring for the soul developed by Jungian psychology fit in well with a Christian perspective, especially when combined with more traditional aids to the soul such as prayer and the sacramental life.

All of this, however, requires an expenditure of effort. Caring for the soul is a form of work—and sometimes also of play. Time must be devoted to the soul, and energy must be invested in it. As we have said, caring for the soul is like caring for a garden, but gardening, however satisfying it is, is also work. In our day, we tend to want someone or something else to do the work for us: the doctor, the priest with his prayers, the psychotherapist with his supposed knowledge. But in the final analysis, if healing comes, it is because we have worked on ourselves.

The compensation for this effort that we must put into our own healing and health is what could be called "ease of movement on the inside." With increased care for the soul, things come more easily from the inside. The ego is now aligned with the creative Center, instead of opposing it, so creative energy flows more easily and naturally. This is the psychological meaning of the following verse, in which we regard waiting for the Lord as the equivalent of inner work:

> but they who wait for the LORD
>   shall renew their strength,
>   they shall mount up with wings
>   like eagles,
> they shall run and not be weary,
>   they shall walk and not faint.
>   (Isa. 40:31)

It should be noted, however, that this faith is not faith that everything will be all right. Naturally we all hope that everything will be all right with regard to whatever maladies or problems we have, and sometimes we have reason to believe that it will be. But everything also may not be all right, and then where are we if our faith requires this as a condition for its existence? The ultimate foundation of faith is not that everything will be all right but that the soul can be sustained whether things are all right or not. From this comes the strength to endure things as they are and grow stronger in the process.

Faith, Hope, and Knowledge

For this reason faith is not to be confused with hope. Of the three gifts Paul mentions in 1 Corinthians 13—faith, hope, and love—hope is the weakest, especially if it is hope that everything will turn out the way we want. In fact, hope can destroy the strength of the soul unless it rests in the ultimate hope that is God. James Stockdale, in recounting how he and many fellow U.S. prisoners survived years of torture and solitary confinement in North Vietnamese prison camps and emerged healthy in mind and body, said that it involved giving up hope. Those who died, he said, were those who hoped. They hoped that the war would end or that there would be a prisoner exchange, or they placed their hopes on this rumor or that rumor. Each time the hopes of these people were disappointed, they became weaker, until they finally died. Those who survived, on the other hand, were those who lived faithfully to their task of life each day and who were also faithful to each other.[11]

The relationship between faith and knowledge remains for us to explore. Jung—who speaks for many people today—believed that the two were incompatible. But as we have noted, faith and knowledge are truly incompatible only when faith is understood as a category of the intellect. When faith is understood as a category of the soul, faith and knowledge are mutually supportive.

This is certainly the attitude of the New Testament. In the Gospel of John, for instance, the word "knowledge" appears more than a hundred times, and the words "to believe" appear ninety-eight times.[12] Faith in God and the knowledge of God are understood here as part of one process.

This relationship between faith and knowledge was well known in the early church. The early Christian philosopher Clement of Alexandria once remarked, "Now neither is knowledge without faith, nor faith without knowledge."[13] And Jung himself, who, as we have seen, expressed a good deal of hostility toward faith, could also see that this opposition was not necessary. The opposition of faith and knowledge, he states, comes about because of an insistence that we *believe.* He writes:

> This conflict is due solely to the historical split in the European mind. Had it not been for the natural psychological

urge to believe, and an equally unnatural belief in science, this conflict would have no reason whatever to exist. One can easily imagine a state of mind in which one simply *knows* and at the same time *believes* a thing which seems probable to one for such and such reasons. There is no cause whatsoever for any conflict between these two things. Both are necessary, for knowledge alone, like faith alone, is always insufficient.[14]

Thus, as stated above, not only are faith and knowledge not in opposition, they are actually mutually supportive. Faith, properly understood, sustains the soul in its search for truth and knowledge; knowledge of the truth in turn confirms faith. Before we know something for certain, we proceed on faith. Jung himself developed his important psychological ideas by having a glimmer of an idea and then, proceeding on faith, persevering in his search for the truth until he found it. In fact, most scientific discoveries can be said to proceed in this way. Albert Einstein, for instance, tells how he spent many years faithfully working out the idea of relativity. The theory came into being very slowly, like a seed that grows silently within the earth, only later breaking the surface of the ground and pushing forth into a full-grown plant, needing nurture along the way. Similarly, his radically new way of understanding the forces and movements of bodies and energy in the universe began as tiny seeds of thoughts. If he had lacked faith in these incipient ideas, they would have perished, but proceeding on the faith that he was on the path to truth, Einstein persevered. It was difficult, and he often became discouraged, but he kept faith with himself and his intuitions until finally one day the whole theory of relativity burst into his mind. Einstein's friend Alexander Moszowski related the story of how the revelation finally came to him:

With infinite precision, the universe and its secret unity of measure, structure, distance, time and space, such a monumental puzzle, was slowly reconstructed in Einstein's mind. And suddenly, as if printed by a giant printer, the immense map of the universe clearly unfolded itself in front of him in a dazzling vision. That is when he came to a sense of peace.[15]

If faith sustains the soul in its search for knowledge, so does knowledge increase faith and bring it to fruition. To *know* the truth is to have faith confirmed and strengthened. To *know* that there is healing in the soul is to have our faith in the healing process confirmed and renewed. To *know* something of God is to have our faith in God enlarged.

The Different Kinds of Knowledge

We cannot understand, however, the relationship of faith and knowledge without also considering the different kinds of knowledge. In our culture most of us suppose that knowledge is, well, simply knowledge; when you know something, it is knowledge, and that is all that is to be said about the matter. But for the Greeks it made all the difference in the world *how* you arrived at your knowledge, for the way you arrived at your knowledge determined what kind of knowledge it was. These distinctions among different ways of knowing and different kinds of knowledge were well known to the writers of the New Testament and in the early church, and different Greek words were used to express different ways of arriving at a truth.

Clement of Alexandria, whom we have already quoted in our discussion of faith, gives us a good description of some of the different Greek words for knowledge.[16] One kind of knowledge, he says, is *epistēmē,* or intellectual knowledge. This word occurs several times in the New Testament in its verb form, for instance, in 1 Timothy 6:4. This kind of knowledge is arrived at by a purely rational process, and faith is not directly involved in it.

Another kind of knowledge cited by Clement is *synesis,* knowledge through logical comprehension. A knowing that comes through logical comparisons or arguments would fall into this category, and, once again, faith would not play much part in it. Still another kind of knowledge comes from the act of observing (*epiginōskō*). If you saw something with your eyes or with mental perception to be a certain way, you would know that fact by having observed it. This word is found in Luke 23:7, in which Pilate observed that Jesus belonged to Herod's jurisdiction. Knowledge acquired by direct empirical observation would fall into this category, and faith, again, is not involved, except insofar as we must have faith that what we see is what is really there.

Still another way of knowing is expressed by the word *horaō,* which means to behold something, often of a visionary sort. Thus we would behold a dream and from the dream arrive at a certain knowledge. In Matthew 2:2 this word is used by the Magi, who said they had "seen" or "beheld" Christ's natal star rising in the East.

But the most important word for knowledge in the New Testament, as Clement points out, is *gnōsis,* or in its verb form, *ginōskō,* a word we have already briefly considered in our discussion of the Gnostics. As we mentioned, the word *gnōsis* is by no means the private property of the Gnostics. To the contrary, it is the main word for knowledge in the New Testament and occurs some forty-five times in the Gospel of John alone. *Gnōsis,* as Clement explains to us, is "the knowledge of the thing in itself."[17] To know some-thing in the manner of *gnōsis* is to have an intimate knowl-edge of it. In fact, *gnōsis* only occurs when we have inner, experiential, intimate knowledge of that which is known. For this reason *gnōsis* is sometimes used as a synonym for sexual intercourse. Thus when we read in Luke's Gospel that Joseph had not yet "known" Mary, the word *ginōskō* is used, as it is in Luke 1:34 (KJV) when Mary says of her preg-nancy, "How shall this be, seeing I know not a man?"

All self-knowledge would be a form of *gnōsis,* as would knowledge of the soul of another person. So also is it with the knowledge of good and evil, a point we shall return to shortly. It will come as no surprise, therefore, to learn that this is the word used in the New Testament for an intimate knowledge of God, as opposed to a merely intellectual knowledge about God. It is also the word used for any mystical or transcendental knowledge.

This kind of knowledge is a partner to faith, and faith is a partner to it. The soul must search for this knowledge; this search is energized by faith, even as the woman with the issue of blood was energized by faith in her search for healing. An intimate knowledge of certain things cannot be had by direct observation nor by rational processes but only by an intimate communion with those things. It is faith that opens up the soul to such communion. It is also faith that enables us to perceive realities that would other-wise not be perceivable. Clement says, "For faith is the ear of the soul."[18] This means that without a certain faith we would not hear God speak to us.

Now we must return to the matter of the knowledge of good and evil. As we have noted, the knowledge of good and evil is also a form of *gnōsis,* or intimate experience with the innermost essence of something. But something changes when it comes to the intimate knowledge of evil: Whereas an intimate knowledge of God, or of the soul of another person, or of our innermost Self, brings enlightenment, intimate knowledge of evil brings darkness and blindness upon the soul. For intimate knowledge of evil is only possible by entering into a relationship with evil, having intercourse with it, as it were, and this leads not to enlightenment but to the obscuring of all the soul's finer faculties. We need to recognize evil when we see it, to observe evil and see what it is like, to be aware of what is evil and what is good—but to *do* evil, to know its innermost essence by entering into it, is the way of death for the soul. This is why God told Adam and Eve not to eat the fruit of the tree of the knowledge of good and evil, for to do so would mean entering into the essence of evil and thus becoming evil. It is also for this reason that Christianity has insisted that Jesus was without sin. The idea, rightly understood, is not to offer up to us a completely blameless person whom we can never emulate, a kind of super Boy Scout who is of a different sort of humanity than we are. Rather, the sinlessness of Jesus can be understood as a sign of his highly conscious and enlightened state, a person whose consciousness was not darkened through psychological intercourse with evil.

Thus the matter of sin is directly related to faith, to knowledge, and to the origin and nature of illness. For sin is an illness of the soul because it partakes of evil, and evil obscures the soul's capacity to know. Because the soul and the body are closely connected, our illnesses of the soul can also translate into illnesses of the body. No examination of the New Testament position on illness and health is therefore complete without taking into consideration its view of sin. It is to this that we now turn.

3

....

Keeping the Soul Healthy

The New Testament can be read for its historical value, for its teachings about social ethics and values, and for its theology. It also contains a great deal of psychology. The writers of the New Testament had a definite understanding of human nature. Jesus, as I think I have shown in my book *The Kingdom Within*, was the world's first depth psychologist. Further, the Old Testament contains the first case histories of the individuation processes in its presentations of the lives of people such as Jacob, Joseph, and Saul.

The psychology of the Bible, however, is not what we would call developmental psychology. Developmental psychology had its beginnings with Freud, who first called our attention to the importance of early childhood influences for our later development. Current psychological trends emphasize the powerful influences upon us as adults of the way our parents treated us when we were children. However, the New Testament, indeed the ancient world generally, had little recognition of the importance of these personal, historical factors in shaping our lives (although Paul did point out in Ephesians 6:4 that parents should not be too severe with their children lest they unnecessarily provoke them to anger or resentment). Instead, the New Testament is concerned with what, in Jungian terms, we would call archetypal psychology. The archetypes are those universal psychic patterns that are fundamental to the personalities of all of us. They belong, as we have noted, to the collective unconscious and are the fundamental ingredients in what we can call human nature. In more biblical language we could say that the psychology of the New Testament is the psychology of the soul: what the soul is like, what is destructive to the soul, and what makes the soul strong and healthy.

Sin and the Soul

What makes the soul strong and healthy is a relationship with God, and what destroys the soul and our relationship with God is said to be sin. If this is true, one might suppose that psychology would take note of sin, analyze its nature, and bring to light its secret workings. But the fact is that the idea of sin is all but totally absent from most psychology today. If, for instance, you consult a standard dictionary of psychology, you will probably not find the word "sin" listed, and if it is, the article about it will be brief and will very likely degrade the idea of sin to its function in inspiring guilt. Consider, for instance, the article on sin in the *Concise Encyclopedia of Psychology*, which, concise though it may be, is more than twelve hundred pages long. The article on sin consists of three brief paragraphs, as follows:

Sin is one of a group of concepts that refer to the violation of laws. Actions that violate human-generated laws are labeled crimes, offenses, or misdemeanors. Sins are actions that violate the laws of God. Experiences of guilt presumably arise from violations of either human-made or God-made laws.

In the Judeo-Christian tradition, the concept of "original sin" serves as an explanatory concept for the qualities of weakness and imperfection found in all human beings.

Actual sin is the term more customarily applied to individual violations of the laws of God. These are often divided into two degrees of seriousness, mortal and venial.

The importance of the concept of sin for psychology rests primarily on the role it plays in the understanding of personal guilt.[1]

The idea seems to be that the notion of sin produces guilt feelings and that this is the only reason it is worth the attention of psychology. Of course there are some good reasons for our rejection today of the idea of sin. Many people have suffered from an overdose of talk about sin from moralists of various religious persuasions whose own lives have turned out to be considerably less than exemplary. Or perhaps in growing up we were exposed to too much moralizing about sin from rigid churches, a moralizing which, instead of enlightening us, left us with morbid guilt feelings and a split personality. Or perhaps our parents used guilt as a way to control us, not only leaving us with false and destructive feelings of guilt but separating us from our natural contact with our creative Center and forcing us to create egocentric defense systems in order to find some way of coping with the psychologically destructive situation.

When the New Testament discusses sin, however, it is not trying to create morbid guilt feelings in us; rather, it is trying to raise the level of our moral and psychological consciousness. Sin, which we can define for our present purposes as our inherent tendency to commit acts of evil, is our foremost inner enemy because sin obscures consciousness and results in the corruption of the soul, and this in turn alienates us from God. Putting this truth psychologically, we would say that sin is the result of an egocentric life, and this life always separates us from the creative life of the Center.

The early church was aware of the spiritual and psychological dangers of sin and of the connection between ignorance, sin, and the corruption of the soul. For the early church, to indulge in sin was to shut oneself off from the light. This only increased the ignorance and darkness of the soul, leading to the soul's loss of contact with God and ultimately to its death. Ignorance tended to darken the soul and lead the soul into sin, and sin further darkened the soul, obscuring the soul's capacity for self-knowledge and understanding. Thus cut off from the light, the soul became separated from God. Since God is the ultimate source of life for the soul, this meant that the soul would die. Consider, for instance, the words of that psychologist-theologian of the early church, Gregory of Nyssa, who wrote in the fourth century A.D.:

> But seeing that ignorance of the true good is like a mist that obscures the visual keenness of the soul, and that when the mist grows denser a cloud is formed so thick that Truth's rays cannot pierce these depths of ignorance, it follows further that with the total deprivation of the light the soul's life ceases altogether; for we have said that the real life of the soul is acted out in partaking of the Good; but when ignorance hinders this apprehension of God, the

soul which thus ceases to partake of God, ceases also to live.[2]

A vivid portrayal in literature of the effects of sin can be found in Oscar Wilde's novel *The Picture of Dorian Gray*. The story centers on the beautiful young man Dorian Gray and an artist who is so taken with Dorian Gray's beauty and attractive personality that he paints a remarkable portrait of him and gives it to him as a gift. Dorian Gray soon discovers that, because of this picture, he is able to do anything he wants, and the effects of his actions will never show in his appearance; indeed, he remains remarkably young and fresh in appearance even as he grows older and in spite of what he might do. Dorian Gray uses this gift, however, as an opportunity to indulge himself in a variety of evil actions. In one instance, he destroys an innocent young woman whom he has seduced into falling in love with him so he can use her sexually. When she discovers the truth that he really despises her, she commits suicide.

Although Dorian Gray's crimes never alter his outward appearance, they invariably show up in his portrait. The picture of the young man that was at first so handsome and pure becomes increasingly hideous and distorted as the number of his crimes against the moral order increases. Indeed, the portrait becomes so horrible to look at that the young man hides it in a secret attic room, only visiting it occasionally to look at it with a morbid fascination. The portrait is in fact a portrayal of his soul. No matter how outwardly beautiful Dorian Gray appears to be, his soul is becoming increasingly ugly and corrupted. At the end of the story, Dorian Gray goes to visit his picture for the last time. Unable to bear any longer the horrible ugliness he sees, he takes a knife and slashes the portrait to shreds, and as he does so he himself dies.

Wilde's novel shows us how sin destroys the soul. It also illustrates the connection between sin and what Fritz Kunkel called egocentricity. Dorian Gray led a completely egocentric life; he acknowledged no power or authority other than his own ego-centered desires. Kunkel believed that our egocentricity is the equivalent of the biblical idea of original sin. It is this that corrupts us; it is the spiritual disease from which we must be cured. Kunkel once made the statement that the closely guarded secret of evil is that the ego is the devil, by which he meant that the ego in its egocentric condition is the door through which archetypal evil enters the soul and eventually comes to possess it. When this happens, Kunkel noted, "the [egocentric] ego, without knowing it, is always fighting on the side of evil and darkness though it pretends to be a servant of light."[3]

The early church made an extensive study of the nature of sin. From this study come the names for the different kinds of sin referred to in the *Concise Encyclopedia of Psychology*. The church, however, made a serious error in its analysis of sin: It decided that fantasies, as well as actions, were sins. Thus if a man or woman had an adulterous fantasy, that constituted a sin in itself even if the person decided not to have the adulterous relationship. If the thought of stealing something popped into a person's mind, that thought in itself was a sin even though the theft was not committed. The result was that sincere Christians felt compelled to repress the shadow, that darker part of our nature that we find objectionable for a variety of moral and other reasons. The shadow, being rejected, was forced into the unconscious, where it lived an autonomous and separated life, leading to a personality split and producing morbid symptoms.

It took Sigmund Freud to bring all of this to light and Carl Jung to help us find a new attitude toward our shadow and a more creative way of relating to our fantasies. But, at least in certain cases, psychology went too far. In liberating us from the morbid guilt that came from repression of our shadow side with its forbidden fantasies, psychology led many people to believe that there was no such thing as sin at all. In fact, such an attitude is so prevalent in the United States today that it seems as if almost anything goes.

The idea of sin in the New Testament, however, has a depth and a psychological validity to it that can lead us into a whole new appreciation of the importance of the matter of sin. It can open the door not to morbid guilt feelings but to an entirely new consciousness, and with this new consciousness can come an increased health for the soul and a deeper relationship with God. On the psychological level, this means an increased capacity to live creatively from the Center, and it means the possibility of liberation from the narrow confines of our egocentricity.

To grasp the subtlety and profundity of the idea of sin in the New Testament, we will need to examine closely the words used there to express the meaning of sin. As the article we quoted from the encyclopedia of psychology notes, most of us identify sin with the breaking of divine laws or commandments. The fact is that the New Testament used eight different words to convey the many nuances and depths of the idea of sin; only one of these words refers to the breaking of divine law. Because this idea of sin is the common one, we will begin with an examination of the role of sin as the breaking of the law. We then will examine the remaining seven words for sin, exploring what they have to teach us about our psychology and about the ways we can keep the soul healthy. Finally, we will examine what the New Testament writers considered the ultimate sin: the sin against the Holy Spirit.

Paranomeō: *To Violate or Transgress the Law*

The idea of breaking the law is expressed in the New Testament by the Greek word *paranomeō*, which means to violate or transgress the law. There are only a few uses of this word in the New Testament. In its verb form, it is found in Acts 23, in which Paul says to the high priest Ananias, "How can you sit there to judge me according to the Law, and then break the Law [*paranomeō*] by ordering a man to strike me?" (v. 3, JB). Use of this word in its noun form (*anomos* or *paranomia*) can be found in Hebrews 10:17, 2 Peter 2:16, and 1 John 3:4. As we have already seen, this word identifies sin with the breaking of God's law, which is our most common perception of the biblical idea of sin: God gave us the moral law; we are to obey it, and if we do not, then we have sinned.

Agnoēma: *To Sin from Ignorance*

The next word we will consider is *agnoēma*, which, literally translated, means "lack of knowledge" and refers to a sin committed in ignorance. As a noun, this word is used only once, in Hebrews 9:7. In its verbal form (*agnoeō*) it can be found in Romans 10:3; 11:25; 1 Corinthians 14:38; and 1 Thessalonians 4:13, but only in Romans 10:3 is the word used with reference to sin. As a verb, this word means "not to understand" or "to sin through ignorance."

In the King James Version and the Revised Standard Version, the noun *agnoēma* is translated as "errors," in the Jerusalem Bible as "faults," and in the J. B. Phillips translation as "sins." Only in the New English Bible is the literal meaning of this word used:

> Under this arrangement, the priests are always entering the first tent in the discharge of their duties; but the second is entered only once a year, and by the high priest alone, and even then he must take with him the blood which he offers on his own behalf and for the people's *sins of ignorance* [*agnoēma*]. (Heb. 9:6, NEB. Emphasis mine)

One wonders why translations other than the New English Bible changed the clear and insightful literal meaning of this word to such neutral translations as "faults" or "sins." To be told that some of our failings are sins committed out of ignorance tells us something important, but to simply say we have a fault does not illuminate us psychologically. Perhaps the explanation lies in the prevailing notion that sin involves being conscious or aware that we are doing something wrong. Can we be censured by God for a sinful act we committed when we did not know that it was sinful?

The Old Testament writers evidently believed that sometimes God held us responsible for our sins even if we were ignorant that we were committing them. We read in Leviticus 4:2: "If any one sins unwittingly in any of the things which the LORD has commanded not to be done, and does any one of them, if it is the anointed priest who sins, thus bringing guilt on the people, then let him offer for the sin which he has committed a young bull without blemish to the LORD for a sin offering."

In the New Testament, God is represented as being sometimes tolerant of sins committed in ignorance and sometimes not. In Acts 17:30, Paul, discussing the fact that people once worshiped God in representations made of gold, or silver, or stone, says that although at that time God "overlooked" ignorance, now "he commands all men everywhere to repent." In Romans 10, Paul seems to come down hard, saying that ignorance is no excuse for sin. With reference to Israel, Paul says, "Brethren, my heart's desire and prayer to God for them is that they may be saved. I bear them witness that they have a zeal for God, but it is not enlightened. For, being ignorant [*agnoeō*] of the righteousness that comes from God, and seeking to establish their own, they did not submit to God's righteousness" (vs. 1–3).

It is worth pointing out that for the ancient Greeks, ignorance was no excuse. It was not a person's intent that mattered, but the act itself. If someone performed a sinful act, that person was responsible even if he was ignorant. In fact, he was responsible even if a god incited him to the action in the first place. The reason was that the person who performed the act was held responsible for his state of mind. If his mind perceived things clearly, his wisdom and moral judgment would not be impaired, even if a god put into his mind the idea of performing an ill-conceived act. Psychologically, this amounts to a belief that the ego's primary responsibility is to cultivate awareness and consciousness; from this all else flows. Therefore sins committed in ignorance are doubly inexcusable: Not only is there the sin to condemn, but also the ignorance.

The following comments by scholar Walter F. Otto are

psychologically insightful and also close to the New Testament point of view. Otto is commenting on the Greek idea that the gods could put certain actions into a person's mind. He writes:

> It is evident that this conception, closely as it binds man to deity, does not signify that he actually lacks freedom. The impression of constraint is all the more ruled out as man's action is predominantly related to the state of his insight. No external will or desire took possession of him when he took the worse course, nor was it that his nobler feeling proved powerless in the face of his cruder inclinations. It is only that his clear perception of the beautiful, the just, and the reasonable—three great realities—was confounded.[4]

Psychologically speaking, this analysis is analogous to the idea of the archetype. The archetypes, those patterns of behavior within us that shape our fantasies and actions in certain specific ways, exert on us a powerful influence, but in the final analysis it is the ego's consciousness and illumination, or darkness and confusion, that determines what act shall be undertaken. And for this state of mind, which is the final determiner of a person's actions, the individual is responsible.

Nature would agree with the biblical and Greek attitude that ignorance is no excuse, for nature is inexorable in its workings. Let us suppose, for instance, that one fine October day we decide to hike in the Sierra Nevada mountains of California. Because the sky is a clear blue and the temperature is rapidly warming up as the sun climbs in the sky, we do not think it is important to bring warm clothing or any form of shelter. All goes well until dark clouds appear over the mountains in the afternoon. Soon, with devastating speed, a storm sweeps over us. The temperature drops forty degrees, and snow begins to fall. We turn and head for safety down the trail, but the snow soon obliterates the trail and we become hopelessly lost. Eventually night falls, the temperature drops even further, and we die from exposure. It does not matter that we could say, "I didn't know that on a day that began so warm and fine in the Sierra Nevada, a storm could come up so quickly." If we act rashly or foolishly from our ignorance, nature does not forgive us.

The same harsh reality prevails in the individuation process. We must grow or perish, become conscious or be spiritually or psychically destroyed, or both. The great task imposed upon the ego is to become aware. If we fail in the task of the development of consciousness, then from the perspective of the Self, we have sinned, for this is the primary function the ego is to perform; and if we fail, certain psychological and spiritual consequences will then result as inexorably as the night follows the day.

We see this psychological truth reflected to us sometimes in dreams in which a dream figure wants to kill us. Such a dream can often best be understood as a statement that this ignorant ego is standing in the way and must be eliminated in favor of a more creative ego. Sometimes a dream even calls for our own execution, even though we have no idea why our death should be demanded. This can be called a "Kafka dream." The novelist Franz Kafka wrote a story called *The Trial*; a gloomy tale, it is still well worth reading for its psychological value. In this story a young man is accused of a crime and told to report to the court. Being an ordinary citizen of good reputation who in his own eyes has done nothing amiss, the young man is certain it is all a mistake and the matter will be cleared up as soon as he finds the court and explains things. The tale goes on from there in the ingenious manner of which only Kafka is capable, but the final result is that the young man is executed, even though he never discovers the nature of the crime of which he is accused. From the psychological point of view, his crime lies in his not knowing, for the primary function of the ego is to know.

To become conscious means to achieve spiritual and psychological insight. It means we become aware of the reasons for our actions, that we see clearly the consequences of our actions and take responsibility for them, and that we achieve some measure of insight into the unconscious workings that lead to those actions. To achieve this consciousness we will need to cultivate the art of self-reflection. We will also need our relationships, for in relationships people react to us, and often their reactions enable us to become aware of things about ourselves which we might otherwise have overlooked. Becoming conscious also means withdrawing projections from other people and taking them back into ourselves. We need to know our own dark side, the shadow, and accept responsibility for it and not compel some other person, race, or group to carry it for us. Thus becoming conscious calls for the cultivation of a certain attitude, an attitude that includes the assumption of psychological responsibility for our actions, moods, and fantasies.

For many of us, this way of consciousness will require that we have another person in our life with whom we can share ourselves on a deep level. This person might be a psychotherapist or a spiritual director or a wise friend or confidant. It is difficult to see ourselves clearly without a mirror to look into; the right person with whom we can share our life can often be that mirror for us, enabling us to see things about ourselves that otherwise we would miss.

In the New Testament the need for consciousness and insight is part of the struggle between darkness and light. This is most clearly exemplified in the Gospel of John, in which darkness and light are seen as spiritual principles, the darkness constantly seeking to swallow the light but never being able to do so. "The light shines in the darkness, and the darkness has not overcome it" (John 1:5). Here the darkness is not the natural darkness of night, which is kindly and beneficent to us, but is a metaphor for spiritual darkness, that is, for unconsciousness. It is this unconsciousness, this inner darkness, that leads us to sin and that first obscures and then destroys the soul. Thus, in early Christianity, sin and not knowing are so close to each other as to be nearly indistinguishable. Gregory of Nyssa once wrote, "For this much perhaps would be plain enough even to the uninitiated, that sin is near akin to darkness, and in fact evil is so termed by Scripture."[5]

But what about obedience to God's will? Is not the word "obedience" one that frequently occurs in the New Testament? How does this obedience fit in with the necessity imposed upon us that we must become conscious? Can we not simply find out what God wants of us and be obedient and dispense with the rest?

The importance of obedience is indeed great, and the sin of disobedience is also great, but as we shall soon see, the biblical idea of obedience does not in any way contradict its insistence that we become conscious followers of the light.

Parakoē: *Disobedience*

Parakoē, usually translated as "disobedience," is the New Testament's third word for sin. It occurs in Romans 5:19,

2 Corinthians 10:6, and Hebrews 2:2. The Jerusalem Bible translates Romans 5:19: "As by one man's *disobedience* many were made sinners, so by one man's *obedience* many will be made righteous" (emphasis mine). It looks as though we are back to the old idea of sin as disobedience to God's law, the parent-child model in which God is the parent who makes the rules and we are the errant children who break the rules. There certainly is such a thing as disobedience to God, but in Romans 5:19, Paul uses Greek words for "obedience" and "disobedience" that get at the *cause* of disobedience as well as the fact of it.

The Greek word that has been translated as disobedience is *parakoē*. Its literal meaning is "imperfect hearing." The verb form of the word means "to fail to listen" or "to hear amiss." The word for obedience in the Greek is *hypakouō*, which means literally "to give ear to," "to hearken," or "to listen." Thus the contrast is between those who listen to God and those who fail to listen or whose capacity for listening is impaired.

The significance of this word for sin can be seen more clearly when we understand the importance the Bible places on hearing. It was the ancient belief that the soul or heart had means of perception just as did the body. The soul as well as the body had the faculties of sight, hearing, taste, smell, and touch. When it came to an awareness of God, the deity was heard more often than seen. In the Old Testament, for instance, when the prophet Elijah was deeply discouraged because Queen Jezebel had succeeded in repressing the worship of Yahweh and the people of Israel seemed to have deserted him, he journeyed through the desert until he reached Mount Horeb, where he found a cave and sat alone in its stillness and cool darkness. Then the story tells us:

And behold, the LORD passed by, and a great and strong wind rent the mountains, and broke in pieces the rocks before the LORD, but the LORD was not in the wind; and after the wind an earthquake, but the LORD was not in the earthquake; and after the earthquake a fire, but the LORD was not in the fire; and after the fire a *still small voice.* (1 Kings 19:11–12. Emphasis mine)

None of the great display of celestial fireworks contained the word of God for Elijah, but from within his own inner stillness Elijah heard the voice of God speaking to him. Renewed and strengthened by God's voice, Elijah regained his courage and returned to the land of Israel to complete his work.

Another of the many Old Testament examples of the voice of God being heard is found in the book of Proverbs. In this case it is Wisdom (Sophia), God's feminine side and cocreator, who is speaking. She begins with these words:

> "And now, my sons, *listen* to me:
>   happy are those who keep my ways.
> *Hear* instruction and be wise,
>   and do not neglect it.
> Happy is the man who *listens* to me,
>   watching daily at my gates,
>   waiting beside my doors."
>   (Prov. 8:32–34. Emphasis mine)

Another important example is from the book of Isaiah, in which God calls Isaiah to his work as a prophet, saying to him, "Whom shall I send, and who will go for us?" And Isaiah replies, "Here am I! Send me." God then says, "Go, and say to this people:

'*Hear* and *hear,* but do not understand;
see and see, but do not perceive.'
Make the heart of this people fat,
    and their *ears heavy,*
    and shut their eyes;
lest they see with their eyes,
    and *hear* with their ears,
and understand with their hearts,
    and turn and be healed."
        (Isa. 6:8–10. Emphasis mine)

This passage from the Old Testament made a great impression on the writers of New Testament. In at least fifteen places in the Synoptic Gospels alone, the admonition "he who has ears to hear let him hear" is repeated in one context or another. Frequently Jesus uses this expression after telling a parable or making a somewhat enigmatic pronouncement. In Matthew 11 Jesus tells the people that John the Baptist is the person anticipated by the prophecies and prophets of old, the one who is to precede the coming of the kingdom of God, the new Elijah returned. After making these comments he concludes, "If anyone has ears to hear, let him listen!" (v. 15, JB).

We also find references to the importance of hearing in the letter to the Hebrews and in the book of Acts. In Hebrews an explanation is given as to why it is so hard to instruct certain people about the meaning of Christ. The text says: "About this [i.e., Christ's meaning] we have much to say which is hard to explain, since you have become *dull of hearing*" (Heb. 5:11. Emphasis mine).

The book of Acts contains several important references to the faculty of hearing. Paul says to the evil people who deny God's word: "You stiff-necked people, *uncircumcised in heart and ears,* you always resist the Holy Spirit" (Acts

7:51. Emphasis mine). Paul's description of his experience on the road to Damascus is also of considerable interest. Paul tells us:

> I was on that journey and nearly at Damascus when about midday a bright light from heaven suddenly shone round me. I fell to the ground and heard a voice saying, "Saul, Saul, why are you persecuting me?" I answered: Who are you, Lord? and he said to me, "I am Jesus the Nazarene, and you are persecuting me." The people with me saw the light but did not hear his voice as he spoke to me. (Acts 22:6–9, JB)

What is noteworthy here is that while all the people with Saul saw the light, only he heard the voice. This indicates that it was his faculty for hearing Christ's voice that was the sign of his apostleship. This fact was not lost on Ananias, who was sent by God to return Saul's sight to him. After healing him, Ananias says, "The God of our ancestors has chosen you to know his will, to see the Just One and *hear his own voice speaking . . .* " (Acts 22:14, JB. Emphasis mine).

It is notable that the author of the book of Acts concludes his document by quoting in full the passage from Isaiah 6 that we have already considered. Evidently he felt this was a fitting climax with which to conclude his message.

We can also note that in the book of Revelation, the admonition to hear the word of God is given at least eight times. In each case the inner or spiritual hearing is emphasized. For example, when John writes the word of God to the seven churches he concludes each message with the words: "If anyone has ears to hear, let him listen to what the Spirit is saying to the churches" (Rev. 2:7, JB; see also Rev. 2:11, 29; 3:6, 13, 22; 13:9).

Neither was the importance of inner hearing lost on the founders of the early church. The brilliant early Christian thinker Tertullian, for instance, carefully distinguished between the ordinary faculty of hearing and the spiritual faculty of hearing. Tertullian noted how often Christ made statements such as, "You shall hear with the ear and not understand" and "He who has ears to hear let him hear." He explains that Christ "was teaching them that it was the ears of the heart which were necessary" if they were to understand.[6]

Clement of Alexandria said much the same thing as Tertullian, but he noted the importance of faith if we are to be able to hear with the inner ear of the soul. He writes:

> "Happy is he who speaks in the ears of the hearing. Now faith is the *ear of the soul*. And such the Lord intimates faith to be when he says, 'He that hath ears to hear, let him hear.' "[7]

The importance of inner hearing was not lost to the ancient Greeks. Homer's *Odyssey* contains a passage to which Clement of Alexandria himself draws our attention after the passage cited above. Homer is discussing the oneness of heart that can come about between a man and a woman. He says that this oneness of heart leads to a kind of inner knowledge that confounds their enemies and rejoices their friends. This knowing comes about through "inner hearing." Homer writes:

> For nothing is greater or better than this, when a man and wife dwell in a home in one accord, a great grief to their

foes and a joy to their friends; but they know/hear it best themselves.[8]

In this quotation, the word translated know/hear is *klyō,* which means "to give ear to" with the connotation of knowing something through the faculty of inner hearing.

The practice of meditation helps us a great deal when we wish to listen to the inner voice. Although there are various kinds of meditation,[9] the essential ingredient is always to find a quiet place and to become quiet within ourselves. This may not be easy to do in today's busy, noisy world. Elijah found he had to go to a mountain and sit quietly in a cave before he could hear God's voice. Jesus had to go into the wilderness, and with the increase in the world's population, wilderness is getting harder to find and more difficult to reach. Our homes are no longer refuges from the world as the noise from busy cities intrudes and someone nearby invariably has the television set going. Fortunately there are still churches and other places of retreat where we can go for meditation. And more than one person I know has discovered that in the middle of the night it is at last quiet, and one can be still and listen. Many people who find themselves awake in the middle of the night and are unable to return to sleep may find that this is a good time to go to their study or some other appropriate place in the house and be still and meditate and listen. In fact, it may be that God wakes us in the night for just this reason. It certainly is easier to return to sleep after we have done our inner work in this way.

There is a reason, however, that more people do not find the silence and listen to the inner voice: They are afraid to do so. The truth is that in our culture we fear silence precisely because something from within *might* speak to us. If our house should be relatively quiet, we quickly fill it up with some kind of sound. We drive home with the car radio on; we leave the car and, entering the silent house, we turn on the television set—just to hear the noise, just so it will *not* be quiet. Or we may avoid the dreaded silence by turning to alcohol or some other drug. We prefer the noise and fear the silence because in that silence the unconscious might make its presence felt. This unconscious will contain all that we have been repressing and denying about ourselves; it will be filled with everything that we have not faced. It is impossible, therefore, to learn to listen to the still small voice of God within, without also coming to terms with the unconscious, that is, becoming comfortable with ourselves. For this we will need times of self-examination. We may need to find a confidant or spiritual guide or psychotherapist. We may find help in a twelve-step group or other support group in which, with the help of others, we can learn to be on better terms with ourselves. Certainly we will have to come to terms with those times in life when we let ourselves and others down. It is to this that we now turn.

To Paraptōma: *Failure to Stand Upright*

To paraptōma is usually translated "trespasses," "sins," "offenses," or "failings." Examples of its use occur in Matthew 6:14, Mark 11:25, Romans 4:25, and Colossians 2:13. In Matthew 6:14 (jb) we read: "Yes, if you forgive others their failings, your heavenly Father will forgive you yours." (In the Revised Standard Version and King James Version, the word is translated "trespasses.") The literal meaning is "a stumbling aside, a false step." It has even been translated, "to fall where one should have stood upright."[10]

The emphasis of this word is not so much on what we did as on what we didn't do. It refers to doing something morally or spiritually inferior in a situation that called for a manifestation of moral or spiritual strength and courage. It is used when we have been less than our best selves. Perhaps in a business situation we see cheating going on—the falsification of records, deception of customers, even embezzlement—but we choose to do nothing. Because we ourselves were not an active part of the deception, we may persuade ourselves that we have not strayed from the path. But, in fact, by not opposing the evil, we may have "fallen where we should have stood upright."

The use of drugs might fall into this category. A psychiatrist friend once explained to me why so many adolescents take drugs: They take them to alleviate guilt, tension, or even boredom. Whenever there is the slightest discomfort, they reach for drugs.

Of course, adults as well as adolescents may reach for some temporary palliative rather than face their discomfort. In either case, if we fail to confront consciously and openly a situation that calls for some kind of creative action on our part, choosing instead an unconscious way out of it, we have fallen into this particular form of sin.

Often such sins appear rationally to be of little consequence, but the unconscious never fails to note them and frequently brings them up in dreams. Ellen, as we will call her, had seen me for psychological and spiritual work for many years. She had also been a member of Alcoholics Anonymous for some twenty-five years. Now that she was doing much better, she saw me on an irregular basis, and our work together resembled spiritual direction as much as it did psychotherapy. One day she reported a short dream: She was having sexual intercourse with a certain man. Our conversation about the dream, which I repeat with her permission, of course, ran something like this:

"Do you know this man, Ellen?" I asked.

"Of course," she answered, looking uncomfortable.

"Well, what about him? It's important that you know what kind of man he was because it makes a difference whom we sleep with in our dreams as well as in our waking life."

"Well," she replied, "like myself he is a member of A.A., but he's nevertheless a terrible liar."

"A liar!" I responded. "Well, you you *like* him?"

"The truth is," she replied, "I can't stand him."

"Well, Ellen," I said, "what on earth are you doing in your dream having sexual intercourse with a man who is a liar and whom you can't stand?"

In answer to this she told me the following story.

It seems that a famous lecturer had come to her church to give a public talk, which she was unable to attend. However, she availed herself of the church's tape library and borrowed the taped copy of the lecture. It was such a good lecture she decided to make her own copy of it, but alas! she made a mistake, and instead of copying the tape, she succeeded instead in erasing the original. She was mortified—so mortified, in fact, that she could not bring herself to tell the tape librarian what she had done but simply returned the blank tape.

It was that night that she had the dream and its meaning was now clear: She had been taken in by a lying voice within her. When we tell lies, it is often as though something inside of us says, "Oh, just say such-and-such; that will get you out of your predicament (or get you want you want)."

An intimate communion with evil is sometimes represented by having sexual intercourse with an evil entity or person. In folklore, for instance, a succubus is a female demon who comes to men at night when they are asleep and has intercourse with them; the offspring of this union is always demonic. An incubus, likewise, is a male demon who comes to have intercourse with women; the resulting child is also demonic. We are reminded of the meaning of "knowing" as intimate knowledge of something (the word *gnōsis* being this kind of knowledge, as we have already considered) and how having sexual intercourse with someone was regarded in the New Testament as conveying an intimate knowledge of that person. Thus to dream of sexual intercourse with a lying man aptly symbolizes "knowing" the evil spirit of lying.

All of this Ellen and I discussed, and when we parted I asked her what she was going to do about the matter of the blank tape. She didn't know what she was going to do then, but she was due to return in a few weeks, and I naturally was curious about how she had dealt with the matter. When she returned she told me the following story:

"I knew as soon as I got home that I had to do something about this tape matter. So the next day I went to the church and told the tape librarian exactly what had happened. Believe me, it took all of my courage to do so, but I also knew that the condition that must be met, if I am to remain sober, is complete honesty, with others and with myself; otherwise I begin to drink again. It took all my strength to do so, but I made my confession to the librarian."

"And what did she say?" I asked.

"Well," she replied, "the amazing thing is that she simply smiled at me and said, 'Oh, don't worry, Ellen, we have nine other tapes exactly like it.' "

This story had a happy ending, but other endings are not always happy, as we will see when we consider the next of our biblical words for sin. First, however, let us consider dreams and their relationship to the health of the soul.

It is worth noting that the Bible placed a great deal of emphasis on dreams. The most noteworthy examples are the five dreams told in the story of the birth of Christ. We are told, "The angel of the Lord appeared to Joseph in a dream and said, 'Get up, take the child and his mother with you, and escape into Egypt, and stay there until I tell you, because Herod intends to search for the child and do away with him' " (Matt. 2:13–14, JB). We need not suppose that a figure with wings, dressed in white, appeared to Joseph in his dream. What we probably have here is the interpretation Joseph placed on a dream in which something numinous appeared to him. The dream may have even been a nightmare that Joseph correctly understood as a message from God (the word "angel" means "messenger") warning him that there was danger to the child and that he should find sanctuary in Egypt.

The Old Testament also tells of many dreams, the most noteworthy example being found in the book of Daniel. It seems that King Nebuchadnezzar has had an impressive dream, but none of his Babylonian dream-interpreters can explain it to him. Desperate to understand the meaning of his dream, Nebuchadnezzar sends for the Hebrew prophet Daniel and asks him to interpret the dream. Daniel tells Nebuchadnezzar that there is a God in heaven who can unravel the meaning of the dream and that this God will make known its meaning to him. Thus closely did Daniel connect dreams and their interpretation with God. Daniel then proceeds to analyze Nebuchadnezzar's dream, but Nebuchadnezzar is still puzzled about just why the dream came to him. Daniel explains that the dream came "in order that the interpretation may be made known to the king, and that you may *know the thoughts of your mind*" (Dan. 2:30. Emphasis mine).

In my book *Dreams and Healing,* I have delved extensively into the meaning of Daniel's words. Suffice it to say here that what the Bible calls "the inmost mind" is what we would call the unconscious. When the prophet says the interpretation comes so Nebuchadnezzar can know the thoughts of his inmost mind, it is the biblical way of saying that dreams come from the unconscious in such a way that, by analyzing the dreams, we can understand the workings of that deep mind within us from which comes illumination and guidance.

The biblical view about the importance of dreams carried over into the early church. Many of the early church leaders discussed dreams and followed their own dreams. In fact, Tertullian once made the comment that the greater part of humanity derived its knowledge of God from dreams. Later, however, when the Christian faith was rigidly codified in creeds and institutions, dreams were generally disregarded. Dream interpretation fell further into disfavor with the coming of the Enlightenment, though certain gifted and original men and women, notably Abraham Lincoln, Robert Louis Stevenson, and Emily Brontë, followed their dreams closely nonetheless.

Around the turn of the century, psychological science took a new look at dreams. Sigmund Freud wrote his *The Interpretation of Dreams* in 1900; not long after that, C. G.

Jung began to publish his writings on the subject. Jung's view on dreams is considerably wider than Freud's and accords well with the biblical view. According to Jung, dreams compensate for deficiencies in our conscious attitude. They emerge from that deeper center within us that he called the Self, presenting us with a view of ourselves that is much larger than the view ordinarily available to the ego. Jung believed it was not too much to say that dreams came from God, since the Self for Jung was like the God within. Jung did not equate the unconscious with God, but he did say that the unconscious was the medium through which God becomes known in the human soul. He believed dreams were an invaluable aid in connecting us to our individuation process because they brought with them inner knowledge and a perspective different from our usual egocentric one, and because they seemed to have a kind of knowledge or feeling for our ultimate psychological destiny. Thus dreams for Jung, as for Joseph and Daniel, were sources of guidance, and the following of dreams brought the gift of an expanded awareness.

Dreams also aid us in awakening and expanding our moral awareness. This is because dreams tell us the truth about ourselves. In their own strange language they represent to us the state of our soul. Ellen's dream is a good example of this: It told her that something was amiss in her soul. A description of the process of recording and understanding our dreams is beyond the scope of this book. Fortunately, there is a growing body of literature on dream interpretation. Christians might begin with my books on dreams or with Morton T. Kelsey's writings.[11] For further books relating to dream work, some of the books by Jungian writers are excellent.[12]

Parabasis: *Taking a False Step*

We now move on to the sin of *parabasis,* a word usually translated as "falling into sin," "disobeying," "breaking the law," or "(committing a) transgression." The literal meaning of the word is "the overstepping or transgression of a line" or "a stepping by the side." Examples of its use occur in Romans 2:23; 4:15; 1 Timothy 2:14; and Hebrews 2:2; 9:15. 1 Timothy 2:14 provides a good example of its typical use: " . . . Adam was not deceived, but the woman was deceived and *became a transgressor*" (emphasis mine).

The image behind this idea of sin is that there are "lines," established by divine ordinance, that are not to be crossed; to disregard these lines is a sin. The law of the Old Testament would be a good example. In the law, all kinds of rules regulate ethical and ritual life; to disregard these laws is regarded as sin, a "transgression" or *parabasis.*

Consider our contemporary penal code. The penal code draws a line around certain kinds of behavior, and crossing over that line constitutes a crime in the eyes of the state. If, for instance, you kill someone violently but without malicious intent, it is considered manslaughter, but if you had malicious intent to kill that person, you have "passed over the line," and your act is reckoned as murder. Or let's suppose you have been pulled over to the side of the road by a California Highway Patrol officer for erratic driving, and, in fact, you have been to a party and have had a few drinks. An alcohol test is administered, and it turns out your blood alcohol content is .07. You are fortunate because you have not yet gone over the line and are not legally guilty of driving under the influence of alcohol. However, if the test had registered .08, you would have been over the line and would have been taken in for driving under the influence of alcohol.

In 2 Samuel 11, David's sin against Uriah the Hittite is a sin of *parabasis*. David's faithful army officer Uriah is married to a beautiful woman, Bathsheba. One day David observes Bathsheba bathing and inquires about her. When he learns she is the wife of Uriah, he contrives to have Uriah placed in the front of a battle where he is likely to be killed. Uriah dies fighting in the service of his king, and David takes Bathsheba for himself. David has gone over the line that regulates human behavior with justice. An outraged Yahweh sends the prophet Nathan to confront David with the heinousness of his crime. Yahweh forgives the repentant David, but the King nevertheless has to pay a penalty for his disregard of the boundaries God has established to limit human indulgence in selfish desires.

The lines that regulate human life, however, are not always drawn as distinctly as they are in the law or the penal code, for many "lines" are codified or written not by humans but by divine ordinance. The lines that regulate human relationships are a good example. Let's take the matter of friendship. The unwritten laws of friendship require that we keep our shadow, our dark side, out of our relationships with our friends. Our shadow may be inflicted on someone other than our friend and not damage our friendship, but if it intrudes into the friendship, it will damage or destroy it. Let us say, for instance, that we decide not to report a certain amount of our income to the Internal Revenue Service. We may have certain rationalizations by which we justify this to ourselves, or we may do it quite blatantly. If our friend should find out what we have done, it is not likely to damage our relationship with that person, unless it does so by lowering our friend's estimation of us. But if we should cheat our friend, our behavior certainly would damage the relationship. We would have gone over the line as far as friendship is concerned, and there would be psychological consequences to our sin of *parabasis*.

There are also lines that invisibly regulate love relationships. Suppose in the course of your work you are regularly in contact with members of the opposite sex. It is quite natural that, despite the fact that you are married, one of these people might be attractive to you. This might lead to a certain amount of friendly banter between the two of you. There surely is no harm in this, and the friendly feelings that exist between the two of you are not damaging to the primary love relationship, even if they should be tinged with a bit of erotic attraction. You can safely return home to your husband or wife without a feeling of guilt or a nagging thought that maybe you are betraying your spouse. But let us say that one day you invite your office friend out to lunch and find yourself enjoying the lunch perhaps a bit too much. Is your action still innocent? Perhaps so, and no doubt you could persuade yourself that there was nothing disloyal to your mate in having lunch with someone. Nevertheless, should your husband or wife happen to ask with whom you had lunch that day, you might find yourself telling something less than the full truth.

Now let us say that it isn't a workday lunch you have arranged with that person you find so attractive, but a dinner at an expensive restaurant. You know that if your husband or wife finds out, there will be hurt feelings, jealousy, anger, and a feeling of betrayal, so you make up an excuse and tell your spouse you had to work late at the office that day. The fact is that you have now crossed over an invisible but very real line, and your secretive behavior, if it should become known, would certainly seriously disturb your primary love relationship. In fact, even if it is not known, it *already* disturbs that relationship because of the lie you felt constrained to tell. Should you further deepen your extramarital relationship by having sexual intercourse with the other person, then of course the disturbance to your primary love relationship would be all the greater, for you would have gone that much further over an important line regulating our love relationships.

Given the importance of the lines that regulate human life, it is not surprising that the ancient Greeks had a goddess who was in charge of such things. Themis was the goddess of all natural and divinely ordained justice and order. (In ancient Greek thought, the natural order and the divine order were virtually indistinguishable.) She was the deity in charge of enforcing all that is valid, right, and needful in human life. She established all those boundaries that limit human beings to their proper sphere and so regulate human life in a manner that is agreeable to the gods and does not instigate their revenge or anger. To assist her in this work, Themis had a sister goddess, Nemesis, whose name means "vengeance." She also had three daughters: Dikē (Justice), Eunomia (Order) and Eirēnē (Peace). If the boundaries laid down by Themis were observed, then justice, order, and peace prevailed, but if they were transgressed, Nemesis rectified maters by taking divine vengeance on the sinners.

Among the rightful limits imposed by the gods on human life was a limit to how much happiness and success a mortal was entitled to, and if this limit was exceeded, one could expect Nemesis to rectify things. The Greeks told the story of King Polycrates, who was tremendously successful in all he undertook. He won all his wars, subdued all his enemies, and lived in great wealth and splendor. However, Polycrates was aware that he was probably exceeding the allowable limit of success in the eyes of the gods. He decided to avert divine vengeance by creating his own misfortune. To do this he took his most valuable possession—an incredibly beautiful jewel—and threw it into the sea. He hoped this misfortune would avert the vengeance of Nemesis. But alas! a fish happened to swallow the jewel; a fisherman caught the fish, found the jewel, and, being an honest man, returned it to the king. This was too much for Nemesis, who, at Themis's behest, went down to Polycrates' kingdom and wrecked everything.

We may smile at this quaint story, but there is truth in it, a truth we recognize in the old custom of knocking on wood when we make a positive statement about our good fortune. The idea is that the devil moves in to wreck good fortune among us mortals when he hears of it, but if we knock on wood, which stands for the wood of the cross of Christ, then the devil has no power.

It does seem a fact that few among us go through life without some dark experience haunting us. In some cases people may live for many years before an illness or some other tragedy touches their lives, but few among us escape entirely.

The fairy tale "The Fisherman and His Wife" further illustrates the reality of the lines we human beings cross only at our peril. It seems there once was a fisherman who was so poor that he and his wife lived in a pigsty. Every day the fisherman went to the sea and fished, and they survived by eating the fish he caught. One day he caught an enchanted fish, a beautiful flounder who had lived in the very depths of the sea. This founder turned out to be an enchanted prince who begged the fisherman to kindly throw him back into the sea. The fisherman, being a good soul, did so. However, when his wife found out about all this, she was furious and commanded the fisherman to go back to the sea, call the flounder back, and ask the flounder for a boon in return for the fisherman's kindness in putting him back into the sea. When the fisherman asked what he should request, his wife said he should ask for a proper house in which to live. So the fisherman did as he was bidden, and when he returned home there was a lovely little cottage to live in instead of the terrible pigsty. It was not long, however, before the fisherman's wife became dissatisfied once again and told her husband to go back and ask for a larger house. Soon she wanted a castle . . . and then that they should become king and queen . . . and then emperor . . . and then the Pope! Each time the fisherman obeyed his ambitious wife's wishes and sought out the fish, the sea was wilder and rougher and blacker. Nevertheless, her wish was always granted, until at last she demanded that she become like God. This finally was too much. When the fisherman returned to his wife, instead of finding her in a fine palace, he found they were back in the pigsty.[13]

This tale perfectly exemplifies the sin of *parabasis*. It is a truth verified in our lives countless times: We persevere in an egocentric course of action just so far, and then we cross over an invisible but quite definite line, at which point our fortunes are violently reversed as those powers of the unconscious that the ancients called deities revolt against our arrogance and excessive greed. Many a dictator, financier, wanton lover—indeed, virtually anyone in search of power and wealth—has crossed that line and ultimately been confronted with a recompense of evil in return for greed. But even those among us who believe they lead moral lives may unwittingly cross over one of life's lines and have to pay the penalty, for as we have seen, not knowing does not save us from the consequences of our errors.

The idea of *parabasis* is that there is a law deeply embedded in God's will, in nature, and indeed in the human heart that is inescapable. It is an idea that runs counter to the prevailing spirit of our times that says that anything goes. We may imagine that we can cast aside the idea of God or divine law, but we cannot ever escape the law of our own nature. Jung once wrote about a seemingly successful man who declared to him, "You can do anything you please as long as the police do not know about it."

However, Jung noted, "He had terrible nightmares and neurotic symptoms because he did as he damn pleased, but he did not connect the two facts. There is a law in ourselves which allows certain things and not others."[14]

This "law in ourselves," Jung noted, is virtually as old as life itself:

Even when you think you are alone and can do what you please, if you deny your shadow there will be a reaction from the mind that always is, from the man a million years old within you. You are never alone because the eyes of the centuries watch you; you feel at once that you are in the presence of the Old Man, and you feel your historical responsibility to the centuries. As soon as you do something which is against the age-long plan, you sin against eternal laws, against average truth, and it will not fit. It is just as if you had eaten something that did not fit your digestive organs. So you cannot do what you please, think what you please, because it might hurt that awareness which has the age of a million years; in a sudden way it will react. It has many ways of reacting, and perhaps you don't feel the immediate impact, but the more you are aware of the unconscious, the more you develop your intuitive sense of law-abiding, the more you feel when you touch the line over which you should not go. If you trespass, you will get a reaction either immediately or indirectly; if you have done the wrong thing, a very powerful reaction may reach you through yourself, or you may just stumble or bang your head. You think that is merely accidental, without remembering what you have done wrong or when you have had the wrong thought.[15]

In our culture there is a strong tendency to want to do away with limits. Some of this may be attributable to the attempt of depth psychology early in this century to liberate our instinctual life from repressive constraints. There was no doubt a need for this, because the restraints from which we needed to be liberated were artificial and destructive ones. In that process of liberation, however, it was overlooked that there are natural and divinely ordained limits that must be adhered to and that can be ignored only at our peril. Furthermore, true freedom consists not in disregarding the just limits imposed upon us but in fulfilling these limits. We find our freedom not in doing whatever we want but in living in accordance with our deepest and truest Self, which is tantamount to serving God. In the words of the Episcopal *Book of Common Prayer,* we need to center ourselves on God, "in whose service is perfect freedom."

The tendency to disregard natural and moral law, however, is deeply engrained in our egocentricity. When our ego takes over, we are prey to what was for the ancient Greeks the worst of all sins. It is a sin also noted in the New Testament, and it is to this that we now turn.

Hubris: *To Set the Ego in Place of God*

Hubris (alternatively, *hybris*) is the only Greek word for sin that has come down directly into the English language. It is usually defined as a state of arrogance and excessive pride. In the New Testament this word appears as both a verb and a noun. As a verb it is usually translated "to treat spitefully," as in Matthew 22:6 (kjv), or "to attack brutally," "to insult," or "to run riot." As a noun it refers to the arrogant setting up of the ego in place of God. The image the word conveys is of an ego that observes no boundaries, limits, or laws but is completely dominated by egocentric attitudes and passions.

For instance, *hubris* is the spirit of the "man of lawlessness" described in 2 Thessalonians 2:4 "who opposes and exalts himself against every so-called god or object of worship, so that he takes his seat in the temple of God, proclaiming himself to be God." We also find the word in its adjectival form in 1 Timothy 1:13 and in the book of Romans where Paul says of the godless and wicked men who suppress all truth that they are "full of envy, murder, strife, deceit, malignity, they are gossips, slanderers, haters of God, insolent [*hybristos*], haughty, boastful, inventors of evil, disobedient to parents, foolish, faithless, heartless, ruthless" (Rom. 1:29–31).

A biblical example of *hubris* can be found in the Old

Testament story of Joseph. The young Joseph, described in Genesis 37:1–11, is a spoiled and arrogant youth. His brothers hate him partly because of their jealousy and partly because he told tales about them to their father. (See Gen. 37:2). When Joseph was seventeen, he had two powerful dreams, one in which he saw his sheaf in the field rising upright and his brothers' sheaves bowing down before his, and a second dream in which he saw the sun and moon and eleven stars bowing down to him. Joseph took these dreams to signify that his brothers should be subservient to him. Naturally, his brothers resented the arrogant way he flaunted his dreams at them, and they plotted revenge. The fact that they went too far in taking revenge constituted their own sin of *parabasis,* but Joseph's sin was *hubris.*

Joseph was cured of his arrogant attitude only by being sold as a slave. It was bitter medicine for the young man, but it often takes bitter medicine to cure us of a particularly malevolent spiritual disease. Only much later in his life, when Joseph was free of his *hubris* and had become a conscious and individuated person through his sufferings, were his dreams actualized in a way he could never have anticipated when he was a youth. This realization took place when Joseph emerged at long last from Pharaoh's dungeon to become the governor of Egypt. (See Gen. 41:39–43.) A great famine swept through all the land, and his starving family had to come to Egypt and ask for food. It was then that his brothers did bow down to Joseph, now Egypt's most powerful figure save for Pharaoh himself, but because of his sufferings Joseph no longer was possessed by the *hubris* that years ago had so antagonized his brothers that they sought to kill him.

The story of Joseph brings us to another aspect of this

matter of keeping the soul healthy. It is implied in the biblical narrative that Joseph used his painful and terrible experiences as opportunities to gain in self-knowledge. The way of consciousness requires that when bad things happen to us, we look first into ourselves to see if we have drawn those experiences upon us or at least contributed to them. Whether we have or not, we must then accept the right attitude toward our suffering. As Kunkel once said, we have to let the suffering ooze through us. In this way our suffering purifies and transforms the soul and purges it of the sin of *hubris.*

The use of the word "hubris" in English, however, no doubt derives not from its use in the New Testament but from the use of this word by the ancient Greeks to express the ultimate sin against the Deity. The following lines from Sophocles will show the way this word is used to express egocentric defiance of the divine order, and the inevitable ruin that follows:

> Of insolence [*hubris*] is bred
> The tyrant; insolence [*hubris*] full blown,
>   With empty riches surfeited,
> Scales the precipitous height and grasps the throne,
>   Then topples o'er and lies in ruin prone;
>   No foothold on that dizzy steep.
> But O may Heaven the true patriot keep
> Who burns with emulous zeal to serve the State.
> God is my help and hope, on him I wait.[16]

A few lines from Aeschylus will further illustrate the way the New Testament use of *hubris* parallels the use of the word in ancient Greece. in *The Eumenides,* the chorus says:

Approve thou not a life ungoverned nor one subjected to a tyrant's way. To moderation in every form God gives the victory, but his other dispensations he directs in varying wise. I give utterance to a timely truth: arrogance [*hubris*] is in very sooth the child of impiety; but from health of soul comes happiness, dear unto all and often besought in prayer.[17]

Hubris brings ruin upon a person because it is the door through which the dread goddess Atē enters into the soul. Atē, though little known to us today, wields a powerful, uncanny, and destructive influence on human life. Indeed her very name means folly, ruin, and sin. At one time it was said that Atē lived on Olympus with the other gods until she played a malicious trick on Zeus, who was so infuriated that he hurled her out of heaven. She fell to the earth, which was thereafter known among the Greeks as "the meadow of Atē." On earth, the goddess roamed to and fro inciting whomever she could to acts of sin and folly that would lead to ruin. She had no power over one's mind if one was reverent of the gods and their will, but those who had succumbed to *hubris* could easily be blinded by the goddess to all moral sensibilities and to the inevitable consequences of a reckless course of action. She could then inspire such a wanton disregard of both human opinion and divine law that people in her grip would plunge into egocentric lives that could only lead to their own destruction. Aeschylus writes of the relationship between *hubris* and Atē:

But the old Arrogance [*hubris*] is like to bring forth in evil men, or soon or late, at the fated hour of birth, a young Arrogance [*hubris*] and that spirit irresistible, unconquerable, unholy, even Recklessness [*Atē*].[18]

In the face of such a sin with its terrifying consequences for the life of the soul, the next word we will consider might seem to be mild, but as we shall see, the danger of this sin can also put the soul to a fearful test.

Hēttēma: *To Fail to Render in Full Measure*

Hēttēma, which occurs in Romans 11:12 and 1 Corinthians 6:7, is usually translated "fault" (KJV), "failure" (RSV), or "defection" (JB). It is related to a Greek word (*hētton*) meaning "less," and its literal meaning is "a diminishing of what should have been rendered in full measure."[19]

The use of this word in the book of Romans shows how the word relates to the diminishing of what should have been rendered in full measure. It is an especially good example because it is contrasted with another Greek word, *plērōma,* which means "fullness." So Paul writes about the Jews,

> So I ask, have they stumbled so as to fall? By no means! But through their trespass [*paraptōma*] salvation has come to the Gentiles, so as to make Israel jealous. Now if their trespass [*paraptōma*] means riches for the world, and if their failure [*hēttēma*] means riches for the Gentiles, how much more will their full inclusion [*plērōma*] mean! (Rom. 11:11–12)

The "failure" of the Jews is clearly seen, from the context of the passage, to be a failure to render in full measure the mission, trust, and gifts God had given them. This turned out to be wealth for the Gentiles since it led to the coming of Christ.

In 1 Corinthians Paul discusses the disgraceful extent to which Christians participate in lawsuits, especially in that they go to pagan courts instead of settling matters themselves. (Paul would be doubly shocked if he lived in our litigious society!) He tells us:

> To have lawsuits at all with one another is defeat [*hēttēma*] for you. Why not rather suffer wrong? Why not rather be defrauded? (6:7)

Or, as we find it in the King James version:

> Now therefore there is utterly a fault [*hēttēma*] among you, because ye go to law one with another. Why do ye not rather take wrong? Why do ye not rather suffer yourselves to be defrauded?

The idea in this passage is that Christians, by going to pagan courts to settle their differences, are being less than they should be. They should have allowed themselves to be defrauded rather than resorting to the public indignity of pagan courts.

We can see from these examples that *hēttēma*, like *to paraptōma*, is a sin more of omission than of commission; it isn't what we did but what we did not do. The possibility of the sin of *hēttēma* arises whenever life brings us a situation that calls for our very best. We may succumb to the temptation of going along with the crowd when the situation called for our strongest moral fiber, or we may give up too easily in the face of difficulty. Life contrives to bring about any number of situations that call for the best in us, but the sin of *hēttēma* often goes unnoticed because our society condones our mediocre behavior. In fact, society may encourage such mediocre behavior because to behave otherwise would make other people feel uncomfortable about themselves. Sometimes, however, God sends us a situation that will make it obvious to ourselves, and perhaps to others as well, that the best in us is required. These can be extremely difficult situations, hence the petition in the Lord's Prayer, "Do not put us to the test" (Matt. 6:13, JB).

When people rise above the sin of *hēttēma,* their heroism often is remarkable. A recent incident in the Sierra Nevada mountains of California illustrates this point. It was winter, and a group of boys from a nearby school rashly ventured out onto the ice of a partially frozen lake. When they were some distance from shore, the ice broke under them and they fell into the icy waters. Three young men by the side of the lake saw the accident. What should they do—watch helplessly from shore or go to the rescue? They chose the latter course, and in attempting to rescue the boys, they themselves drowned. They were surely "put to the test." Those of us who read the account of this tale were grateful that we were not the ones who had to make that difficult choice. Perhaps the young men would have chosen more wisely in terms of their own safety by remaining on the shore, but no one can ever fault them for not giving of themselves in full measure.

A similar story was told to me by a Jewish client. I relate it here with his permission. In the course of our early work together, I was still gathering information about his family and background and asked about his extended family. "I have no extended family," he answered. I expressed surprise, and he explained, "They all died in the Holocaust . . . except for one aunt." He explained how it was that his aunt lived when the others died. At dusk, somewhere near the Russian-Polish border, the Nazis rounded up the Jews

108

of a certain village, intending to shoot them. Among the group of Jews was my client's aunt, who was carrying her infant child. As she passed the German soldier assigned to shoot her and her child, the soldier whispered to her, "When I shoot, run!" He shot into the air, and the woman ran into the forest and escaped in the darkness. She made her way into Russia and somehow managed to survive the war. The German soldier could easily have shot the woman, and who would have blamed him? If challenged later, he could have said, "All of us soldiers had to shoot, or we would have been shot." Or, "If I had not shot her, someone else would have." Or, "I was following orders." The fact is that this soldier did *not* shoot. He rendered in full measure what was required of him and therefore avoided the sin of *hēttēma,* while the other soldiers, in all likelihood, were not even aware that they were sinning.

What became of the German soldier? Was his act seen, and was he himself executed? We will never know. He goes down in history as one of those anonymous people who lived and died gruesome lives during World War II. Yet if he died, he did not die unknown. His act lived on in my client's family, and the story was passed along to me, and I pass it along to the readers of this book. It is not too much to say that in the soldier's act and his avoidance of *hēttēma* under the most difficult of circumstances, he individuated, or at least took a huge step forward in the great process of becoming his true Self. When this happens to someone, that person has an effect on others. That soldier's consciousness now affects our consciousness.

Was the soldier a Christian? We have no way of knowing. Had he "accepted Christ"? We have no way of knowing that, either. Yet it is hard not to believe that this man was known to God and accepted by God for his act.

Named or unnamed, Christ was with him and in him as he made his decision and spared the life of the innocent woman and child.

Turning to the Bible, we find an example of *hēttēma* in the story of Peter's denial (Luke 22:54–62), with parallels in all three other Gospels. Jesus has been seized by his enemies and led off to trial and ultimate crucifixion. Peter tries to remain anonymous, but a woman recognizes him as one of Jesus' disciples. She peers at Peter and says to the people around them, "This person was with him too" (v. 56, JB). But Peter denies that he has ever known Jesus. This happens three times. After the third denial, a cock crows. Then Peter remembers that Jesus had said to him, "Before the cock crows today, you will have disowned me three times" (v. 61, JB). Peter then goes outside and weeps bitterly.

Peter's sin was in failing to give in full measure what should have been given. The situation called for loyalty and courage, even if it meant endangering himself. Peter put his egocentric concern for his own safety over his loyalty to Jesus and his faithfulness to all that Jesus called him to be. This was *hēttēma,* and when he was faced with his own darkness by the crowing of the cock, he wept bitterly.

Peter wept because he instantly recognized his sin. As emotionally distressing as his betrayal of Jesus was, it led him into greater consciousness of himself. Now Peter really saw his egocentric side—his darkest shadow. This bitter self-confrontation led to a new, though humbling, awareness of himself through his failure to give in full measure what should have been given. Truly, we often—perhaps usually—awaken to consciousness more through our sins than through our successes, provided that we have developed the habit and practice of self-scrutiny.

Note Peter's shame. There is false shame and true

shame. Some people, especially those who were made to feel ashamed of themselves when they were small children, have to overcome the damage that false shame has done to them. But there is also a genuine shame, a shame that belongs to us. The Greeks, in fact, even had a goddess of shame. Her name was Aidōs, and it was her province to send to each person that individual's allotment of shame. True shame comes specifically when we have committed a sin of *hēttēma*. Where there is true shame, there also is the sin of *hēttēma,* and where there is this sin, there also is the shame, although in some cases it may be buried in the unconscious. But not so with Peter. It is true that he denied Jesus, but he did not go so far as to deny his shame at what he had done. And it was this courage to face his shadow, to see the shamefulness of his act of *hēttēma* that brought Peter through his experience and led him to his true Self.

Psychologically, our egocentricity is always at the root of sin. In our desire to protect ourselves at all costs and to further our own egocentric ambitions, we continually fail to give to life what should have been given in full measure. Furthermore, when we are confronted with our psychological and moral failures, we will usually defend ourselves with self-serving excuses. We may also wind up associating with people of like mind, since people of greater consciousness and moral integrity make us feel uncomfortable. We may be unaware of the roots and causes of our behavior, of course. Awareness of what we are doing is the beginning of our salvation, but it is also quite painful. We often prefer the darkness of not knowing to the sometimes agonizing scrutiny of the light. But as we have already seen, not to know is no excuse when it comes to the spiritual world. Indeed, *agnoēma,* as we have seen, is a sin in itself.

As long as we are egocentric, we are bound to fall into sin; only if we live from the Center, which for the Christian is Christ, can we give to life the full measure that it requires from us. But living from the Center means being related to the Center, being someone who is, as the New Testament would put it, "on the mark," for to miss the mark is inevitably to err. Hence sin as a "missing of the mark" is the most important of all the New Testament words for sin. It is to this that we now turn.

Hamartia: *To Miss the Mark*

Of all the words for sin in the New Testament, the most important and most frequently used is *hamartia.* As a noun it is found in Matthew 1:21; John 9:41; Romans 7:7, 17, 20; 2 Corinthians 5:21; and Hebrews 9:26, as well as many other places. In its verb form (*hamartanō*), it can be found in Matthew 18:15; John 5:14; 1 Corinthians 15:34; and Titus 3:11. The word *hamartēma,* a first cousin to *hamartia,* can be found in Mark 3:28; Romans 3:25; and 1 Corinthians 6:18. It is usually translated simply as "sin," or, in its verb form, "to sin." Paul says in his discussion of the law: "What then shall we say? That the law is sin [*hamartia*]? By no means! Yet, if it had not been for the law, I should not have known sin" (Rom. 7:7). Its literal meaning, however, as we noted in chapter 1, is "the missing of a mark or aim," or, as a verb, "to miss the mark."

The importance of the idea of missing or hitting the mark is emphasized by the use of other words similar in meaning to *hamartia.* One of these is the word *astocheō,* which we find in 1 Timothy 1:6 and 2 Timothy 2:18. This word is usually translated "swerving" or "having swerved" (KJV, RSV), or "falling short" (NEB), or "gone off the straight course" (JB). However, like *hamartia,* its literal meaning is "to miss the mark."

In contrast, *tygchanō,* a New Testament word for salvation, means "to hit the mark," or, secondarily, "to obtain": "Therefore I endure everything for the sake of the elect, that they also may obtain [*tygchanō*] salvation in Christ Jesus with its eternal glory." (2 Tim. 2:10).

Hamartia, hamartanō, and *tygchanō* were the words used by ancient Greek archers for hitting the center of the target. The Greeks saw a natural analogy between an archer missing the target and a human being swerving from the right path in life. An understanding of the Greeks' use of this word will amplify our understanding of its use in the New Testament. Walter F. Otto pointed out the connection between the use of this word in archery and its use by the Greeks to represent acting rightly in life. He wrote, "We know that the Greeks habitually pictured recognition of what is right under the image of an accurate bow-shot."[20]

Consider, for instance, the use of *hamartanō* by Aeschylus. In Aeschylus's *Agamemnon,* the prophetness Cassandra is speaking out against the crimes committed in the house of Agamemnon, the sacrifice by Agamemnon of his daughter, Iphigenia, the vengeful murder of Agamemnon by his wife, Clytemnestra, and the murder in turn of Clytemnestra by their son, Orestes. Cassandra then asks herself of her prophecy: "Have I missed the mark [*hamartanō*] or, like a true archer, do I strike my quarry? . . . Bear witness upon thine oath that I do know the deeds of sin [*hamartia*], ancient in story, of this house."[21]

A central Greek idea is that the inability of the archer to hit the target lies in a fault in the character or consciousness of the archer. The case of Oedipus is a good illustration.

Oedipus had sexual intercourse with his mother and killed his father. Separated from his parents at birth, as an adult he had no way of knowing of his blood ties to these people. His ignorance, however, made no difference, and his acts were reckoned to him as sins. He says to his accuser, Creon:

> O shameless railer, think'st thou this abuse
> defames my grey hairs rather than thine own?
> Murder and incest, deeds of horror, all
> Thou blurtest forth against me, all I have borne.
> No willing sinner; so it pleased the gods
> Wrath haply with my sinful race of old,
> Since thou could'st find no sin in me myself
> For which in retribution I was doomed
> To trespass thus against myself and mine.[22]

Turning now to the great Greek philosopher Aristotle, we find a clear example, in his use of *hamartia,* of the connection in the Greek mind between sin and not knowing, or unconsciousness. The sin derives from an insufficient knowledge of life conditions that in other circumstances might, in fact, have been known by the one who sinned. If the individual is not responsible for his ignorance, then the moral consequences of his sin are lessened, but it remains sin nonetheless because he missed the mark.[23]

Euripides echoes that sentiment. In his *Hippolytus,* the goddess Artemis says to Theseus, who has destroyed his son, Hippolytus, because he erroneously supposed that the youth had slept with Theseus's wife:

> Deep thy sin
> ....
> But thy transgression [*hamartia*]
> Thine ignorance from utter sin redeems.[24]

114

Interestingly enough, less than a century before Euripides wrote his play, the Chinese philosopher Confucius also compared the idea of sin to the failure of an archer to hit the target and noted that the archer's failure lay in himself. He tells us:

> In archery we have something like the way of the Higher Man. When the archer misses the center of the target he turns around and seeks for the cause of the failure in himself.[25]

What we see here is the direct relationship between sin and unconsciousness. To be unconscious, to be in the dark or lacking insight into oneself and the circumstances of life, means that we will inevitably miss the mark and thus will sin. Just as sin darkens and obscures consciousness, so sin can ultimately be overcome only with the increase of consciousness. Sin and unconsciousness are inseparable, the one always existing with the other. The person who is unaware of the truth about herself will inevitably miss the mark in life and hence will sin. Therefore, only insofar as we pursue a life dedicated to self-knowledge and illumination can we hope to avert some of the effects of sin.

But what if we steadfastly refuse to acknowledge the truth about ourselves? This question leads us to the final consideration in our analysis of sin and the health of the soul: the matter of the sin against the Holy Spirit.

The Sin Against the Holy Spirit

This is the ultimate sin, the sin unto death. Jesus declared, "Therefore I tell you, every sin [*hamartia*] and blasphemy will be forgiven men, but the blasphemy against the Spirit will not be forgiven" (Matt. 12:31).

In 1 John 5:16 (KJV) we read, "If any man see his brother sin a sin which is not unto death, he shall ask, and he shall give him life for them that sin not unto death. There is a sin [*hamartia*] unto death. I do not say that he shall pray for it."

Now the Holy Spirit, as we know from John's Gospel (14:17; 15:26; etc.), is the Spirit of truth. The sin against the Holy Spirit is a refusal to face the truth and therefore is an avoidance of becoming conscious and a persistence in the way of darkness and unconsciousness. This refusal to become conscious of the truth, especially the truth about oneself, thwarts God's purposes in one's life. This is the deadly sin against the Holy Spirit, for it amounts to nothing other than the choice of the darkness over the Light. "The light shines in the darkness," we read in John's Gospel (1:5), "and the darkness has not overcome it." But what if we ourselves belong to the darkness? Then there can be no Light in us. Indeed, the refusal to become conscious was the sin of the Pharisees, for which reason Jesus said of them, "they are blind guides. And if a blind man leads a blind man, both will fall into a pit" (Matt. 15:14). And again,

> Woe to you, scribes and Pharisees, hypocrites! for you cleanse the outside of the cup and of the plate, but inside they are full of extortion and rapacity. You blind Pharisee! first cleanse the inside of the cup and of the plate, that the outside also may be clean. (Matt. 23:25–26)

Jesus uses here the symbol of cleaning a cup: The most important part to clean is the inside of the cup, for it is the inside that will hold the next liquid we drink from it, and if it is left dirty we will take the dirt into ourselves. The image of the cup is an image of our selves. The most important part of ourselves is what lies within us. Washing the outside of the body is nothing in importance to ministering to the cleanliness of the soul. As long as we concentrate only on the image of ourselves that we present to other people (the *persona,* in Jung's language), we are like the Pharisees who clean only the outside of the cup. Cleaning the inside of ourselves means dealing with all within us that we have left in an unconscious condition. It means making conscious our real nature with all of its lower motivations; it means coming to know the nature of the shadow. This done, our eyes are open, we see clearly, and a moral life can ensue from this awareness and self-knowledge. Otherwise we will be, like the Pharisees, "blind guides."

To choose the way of darkness, John tells us in his Gospel, is to choose the way of death. The soul lives through participation in the Light; it dies when it lives in the darkness of sin and ignorance. According to John, we are living in this lifetime toward the Light or the darkness, toward greater life or death. To live in ignorance and darkness is to be dead within oneself, for the soul can die even before the body dies. Jung once wrote about people who appear to be alive and walking about in the world, but are in fact dead in their souls because their souls have been deprived of the light that comes from self-knowledge:

> It is death to the soul to become unconscious. People die before there is death to the body, because there is death in the soul. They are mask-like leeches, walking about like spectres, dead but sucking . . . . You can succeed in going away from your problems, you need only to look away from them long enough. You may escape, but it is the death of the soul.[26]

117

Conclusion:
The Psychology of Healing—
A Christian Perspective

Anyone who has hiked through the mountains knows that from time to time a hiker stops and looks back over the course she has taken. So we who have been exploring the realm of healing in the New Testament and in psychotherapy today can now pause and look back over the way we have come, and also forward to the future. We began by examining the several causes of illness as we find them exemplified in the New Testament. We saw that illness can result from a wrong attitude toward ourselves and life, as exemplified in the story of the man by the pool of Bethzatha, and we noted that such attitudes were regarded in the New Testament as a form of sin. We compared these cases of illness with psychosomatically engendered illnesses, which are also the result of a faulty life attitude. The cure for such an illness therefore would involve a change in attitude and a new and more creative way of facing life. In the case of the man by the pool of Bethzatha, he had to leave the pool where he had languished for thirty-eight years and face life as a well person. We also saw, however, that in some cases a person is ill because the illness is "fated"; that is, factors beyond a person's control have inflicted the illness upon him. We have noted that this appeared to be the case with the man born blind, but even then we saw that the power of God can be manifested in that person's life, bringing about a cure of the illness or a triumph of the human spirit, or both, when it is aided by God.

Our attention then turned to the story of the woman with the issue of blood. Here we saw that sometimes an illness is an integral part of our process of individuation. We noted that some illnesses persist until we have been led to a certain spiritual destination or goal; then they are alleviated in such a way that, as a result of our search for healing, we have become entirely new and more whole people.

Most important of all, we observed that the New Testament also describes a variety of illnesses of the soul and regards these illnesses as of more concern than illnesses of the body. This is because the soul carries our fundamental Self, that mysterious, enduring part of us that is able to survive death and achieve union with God. Jesus warned us, "Fear not them which kill the body, but are not able to kill the soul: but rather fear him which is able to destroy both soul and body in hell" (Matt. 10:28, KJV).

Now, the health of the soul is put in jeopardy by sin. As we have seen, the New Testament used eight different words to express the manifold nature of sin. Freedom from sin is accomplished by the grace of God, but for the grace of God to operate effectively, two conditions under which sin flourishes must be overcome: our hardness of heart and our blindness of mind or understanding.

Hardness of heart destroys our capacity to understand because enlivening emotions cannot penetrate into the hardened soul. Jesus says to those who are incapable of understanding the meaning of his actions and sayings: "Do you not yet perceive or understand? Are your hearts hardened? Having eyes do you not see, and having ears do you not hear?" (Mark 8:17–18).

Jesus frequently referred to the Pharisees as "blind guides." He says of them, "Can one blind man guide another? Surely both will fall into a pit? . . . Why do you observe the splinter in your brother's eye and never notice the plank in your own? How can you say to your brother, 'Brother, let me take out the splinter that is in your eye,' when you cannot see the plank in your own? Hypocrite! Take the plank out of your own eye first, and then you will see clearly enough to take out the splinter that is in your brother's eye" (Luke 6:39, 41–42, JB).

From the viewpoint of a religiously oriented psychotherapy, the sins the Bible describes can be understood as sins of egocentricity. Egocentricity occurs when the ego sets itself up as the center of the personality in place of the real, God-given Center. The goal of the egocentric ego is always to protect itself and further its own ambitions for security or power. Thus the egocentric ego loses a relationship with the true Center, which is always creative and free. Accordingly, the ego loses its relationship with God, who is the author of this creative Center. Characteristic of the egocentric ego is its hardness and rigidity, from which comes its resistance to change and its lack of creativity. The egocentric ego also stubbornly refuses insight, since insight into its various psychological mechanisms would make it more difficult for the ego to maintain the rigid system of defenses and power motives that it feels

121

(erroneously) are essential for its existence. The more un-aware we are of our egocentricity, the greater is its power over us, which results in our being cut off from our true Selves, our capacity to love, and the source of healing within us. Consequently all spiritual and psychological healing must involve a breaking down of our egocentric-ity, with a corresponding increase in our power to see and feel the truth, especially the truth about ourselves. This is not to say, however, that the ego is by nature demonic. The ego is created by God and is an essential part of our wholeness. Its proper function is to know, learn, observe, understand, and, when so called upon, to suffer. It is to be the means through which the creative Center is expressed in life. Thus understood, it is a vital part of our totality. It stands in the way only when its proper function has been distorted by egocentricity.

Thus while freedom from sin is ultimately the gift of God, a necessary precondition for receiving this gift is that our eyes are open to the truth and our hearts open to feel-ing and to whatever suffering should prove to be our lot in life. It is important to remember the importance of suffer-ing, because psychological insight and spiritual under-standing can hardly be realized without it. This is why Paul said his life changed fundamentally because he was crucified with Christ. (See Gal. 2:20.) While not all suffer-ing leads to spiritual and psychological growth, still it re-mains a fact that, in many instances, understanding comes about only through a certain amount of suffering. This truth was beautifully stated by the Greek playwright Aes-chylus, who once wrote, "He who learns must suffer, and even in our sleep pain which will not forget falls drop by drop upon the heart, and in our despair, against our will, comes wisdom by the awful grace of God."[1]

The idea that there is a larger center of the personality than the ego is not found in most contemporary psychology. We owe this idea mostly to Jung. For this reason alone Jung's psychology, while not flawless, is of great importance for anyone interested in a truly religious psychology. The best exposition of the nature of egocentricity, however, is found not in the psychology of Jung but in the writings of Fritz Kunkel. Kunkel embraced Jung's idea of the Self as a second, and greater, center to the personality than the ego, but he emphasized that as long as the ego is in an egocentric state it will be cut off from this creative Center and will live in a state of morbid isolation. Kunkel regarded egocentricity as the psychological equivalent of original sin: Passed on from generation to generation, it is a condition that pervades the human race. Although an in-depth study of Jung and Kunkel is beyond the scope of this book, their relevance for understanding healing in the New Testament and for understanding the psychological outlook of Jesus and Paul can hardly be overestimated.[2]

A close examination of the New Testament shows that it anticipated both Jung and Kunkel in many ways. In the references to spiritual blindness and hardness of heart, and in the complex and subtle discussion of sin, the New Testament describes for us the essence of egocentricity. The idea of the Self or Center as the larger or greater center of the personality was anticipated in the idea of the God within. In addition to Paul's famous statement in Galatians 2:20 that it is no longer he who lives, but Christ who lives within him, there are many other examples throughout the New Testament of the belief in the immanence of God within the soul.

Today we hear little of the reality of the God within, of the Christ who lives in the soul and is our true Center, perhaps because we live in an extroverted and materialistic era, whereas Christianity was born in an introverted era in which people believed in spiritual reality. The cultural attitude today is that all reality is outside of ourselves; only concrete, material things are real, and inward psychological realities are "only psychology." The difference between the ancient and modern points of view is nicely illustrated by the way in which Luke 17:20–21 is rendered in contemporary biblical translations. In these verses Jesus answers the Pharisees, who demand to know when the kingdom of God will come, by saying: "The Kingdom of God cometh not with observation: Neither shall they say, Lo here! or, lo there! for, behold, the kingdom of God is within you." That, at least, is the way the King James Version of the Bible translates the text, but most modern translations render it, " . . . the kingdom of God is *among* you" (emphasis mine). The difference between the translations "within you" and "among you" points to the change from an introverted and soulful perspective to an extroverted perspective that sees reality only outside of oneself.

What did Luke really say? The Greek expression is *entos hymōn,* an expression that can mean either "within" or "among." The extroverted attitude chooses "among"; the introverted attitude chooses "within." But which meaning did Luke really have in mind? Probably both, for the mystery of Christ is that Christ is both within and among, inner and outer. Psychologically, this means that the Center not only is within us but also exists between us and another person as the vital center of relationship, and among the members of a creative and related group in which Christ functions as the Center. Jung primarily stressed the inner reality of the Center; he once wrote that the innermost core of every unit of life is God. For Kunkel, on the other hand, the Center has no boundaries and can be manifested outside of us as well as within us, for it exists wherever relationship exists, be that the relationship of the various parts of our selves or the relationship between us and other units of life. Relationship is key here, for although times of solitude are essential for us so we can commune with and relate to our inner life, it is also true that the Real Self emerges only when we are in relationship with our fellow human beings. This point of view is expressed by Jesus when he says, "Where two or three are gathered in my name, there am I in the midst of them" (Matt. 18:20). Much the same idea is expressed in John 17, where Jesus talks of the oneness that exists among himself and the disciples.

The fact that the Center exists both *within* and *among* answers the objection some people have that psychology is self-absorbed and that an interest in psychology indicates a lack of social concern and relatedness. To the contrary, a psychologically whole person will be involved in the whole of life and will live in relationship with his fellow human beings.

Within these pages we have used the New Testament expression "the mystery of Christ." This word "mystery" requires some explanation. For us today, a mystery is something we don't understand, a puzzle to be solved. The New Testament word translated "mystery," however, is the Greek word *mystērion,* which means something that can be known only by being experienced in a personal and intimate way. The word conveys the meaning of an esoteric or mystical knowledge that can be comprehended only by those whose understanding has been enlightened by personal experience with the source and object of its knowing.

Thus Christ confounds our usual ideas of within and without, for Christ is both within and without, both in us and among us. If Kunkel is right, this corresponds psychologically to the Real Self, our true Center from which all true healing ultimately comes.

Every medical doctor knows that the body has the capacity to heal itself with its own internal systems of self-regulation and defense against infection. If the body has lost its capacity for self-healing, the greatest skill of the doctor is of no avail. Likewise, the psychotherapist knows that the psyche has the power to heal itself, for the psyche has a Center that brings about the healing and the creative evolution of the personality.

As we have noted, for the Christian this Center is indistinguishable from Christ, though the creative Center works in believers and unbelievers alike, provided that they have the correct spiritual attitude and are willing to grow through the process of becoming whole. It seems that even as Jesus showed little interest in people's belief systems, healing them regardless of their theology, so also today healing is generated within people who have little concern for doctrinal beliefs but great concern for their state of enlightenment and their ability to become free of their egocentricity.

In the end, though, the deepest healing for us transcends our welfare in this world. Healing that springs from the Center not only restores the mind and body to health but also renders the soul sound, creative, and incorruptible. It is not too much to suggest that the creation of such an undivided and full realized Self may resonate into a life beyond this earthly existence. Such, at least, was the faith of the New Testament, which saw this as the ultimate healing.

Notes

Chapter 1.
The Meaning of Illness in the Gospels and in Psychotherapy Today

1. I believe in the use of inclusive language, but it is awkward to repeatedly substitute expressions such as "he and she" or "him and her" for the old, sexist use of the male pronoun to represent both sexes. To resolve this difficulty I will use sometimes "he" and sometimes "she" to represent both sexes. Further, for the sake of preserving the original language, I have not altered quoted material to make the language more inclusive. I would invite the reader, however, to mentally substitute inclusive language when reading the quoted matter.

2. Scholars debate the authorship of the fourth Gospel. For the sake of convenience, we will refer to the author as "John," although in fact it is doubtful that the Galilean fisherman John, one of the twelve disciples, wrote this sophisticated document.

3. Old Testament references to Satan are 1 Chronicles 21:1; Job 1:6–9, 12; 2:1–4, 6–7; and Zechariah 3:1–2. For more on this subject, see Rivkah Schärf Kluger, *Satan in the Old Testament.*

4. For a good treatment of the connection between sin and illness in the Old Testament, see Conrad E. L'Heureux, *Life Journey and the Old Testament: An Experiential Approach to the Bible and Personal Transformation.*

5. From "The Order for the Visitation of the Sick" in *The Book of Common Prayer.* Emphasis mine.

6. Ibid.

7. For a complete discussion of these and other issues raised by the idea of reincarnation, see my book *Soul Journey: A Jungian Analyst Looks at Reincarnation.*

8. Sophocles, *Antigone,* line 236.

9. See *Fritz Kunkel: Selected Writings,* ed. John A. Sanford.

10. Statement made by Robert P. Sedgwick in conversation.

11. Aeschylus, *Agamemnon,* line 1000.

12. Jesus says to her, "Daughter, your faith has made you well." The Greek is *sesōken,* which is the third person singular perfect active of *sōzō.*

Chapter 2.
Faith and Knowledge in the Healing Process

1. See Lancelot Law Whyte, *The Unconscious Before Freud: A History of the Evolution of Human Awareness.* For examples of how

the knowledge of the unconscious was anticipated in the New Testament, see Gerd Theissen, *Psychological Aspects of Pauline Theology.*

2. C. G. Jung, *Aion: Researches into the Phenomenology of the Self,* paragraph 269.

3. Jung, *Civilization in Transition,* paragraph 171. Emphasis is Jung's.

4. Ibid., paragraph 551. Emphasis is Jung's.

5. Ibid., paragraph 853.

6. C. G. Jung, *Psychology and Religion: West and East,* paragraph 763. Emphasis is Jung's.

7. Examples occur in Matthew 18:6; 27:42; John 3:15, 16, 18. The coupling of *pisteuō* with *eis* (into) is the most frequent usage.

8. See my edited volume, *Fritz Kunkel: Selected Writings,* pp. 233ff.

9. I favor this translation for its use of "within you." An alternative translation is "among you." See my book *The Kingdom Within: The Inner Meaning of Jesus' Sayings,* pp. 32–33.

10. Plato, *Apology,* paragraphs 29E, 30D. The Greek for "care of the soul" is *epimeleia tēs psychēs.*

11. Admiral Stockdale's best account of his prison experience is in "The Melting Experience," an article he wrote for *National Review* (25 December 1981). I summarize it in *Fritz Kunkel: Selected Writings,* pp. 329ff. It is an astounding account of the

power of the soul to survive and remain healthy amidst the most difficult experiences.

12. The words in the New Testament for "to believe" (*pisteuō*) and for "faith" (*pistis*) come from the same root: *pith-*. This root implies the image of binding. To believe or to have faith is to be bound or persuaded to a person or idea.

13. *The Stromata* 5.1.

14. From "Yoga and the West," in *Psychology and Religion: West and East,* paragraph 864.

15. Louis de Broglie, Louis Armand, and Pierre-Henri Simon, et al., *Einstein,* p. 21.

16. Clement of Alexandria, *The Stromata* 2.17.

17. Ibid.

18. Ibid., 5.1.

Chapter 3. Keeping the Soul Healthy

1. *Concise Encyclopedia of Psychology,* s.v. "sin." Emphasis mine.

2. Gregory of Nyssa, "On Infants' Early Death," in *Nicene and Post-Nicene Fathers of the Christian Church,* vol. 5, p. 376.

3. *Fritz Kunkel: Selected Writings,* p. 387.

4. Walter F. Otto, *The Homeric Gods,* p. 185. See also the discussion by E. R. Dodds, *The Greeks and the Irrational,* pp. 3–4.

5. Gregory of Nyssa, "Letters I," in *Nicene and Post-Nicene Fathers of the Christian Church,* vol. 5, p. 527.

6. Tertullian, *Against Marcion* 4.19.

7. Clement of Alexandria, *The Stromata* 5.1. Emphasis mine. The quotation is from Matthew 11:15, KJV.

8. Homer, *Odyssey* 6.185.

9. For more on methods of meditation based on the Bible, see Morton T. Kelsey's book *The Other Side of Silence: A Guide to Christian Meditation.*

10. This is the translation given by the Rev. Samuel G. Green. See Green's *Handbook to the Grammar of the Greek New Testament,* p. 381.

11. See, for example, Morton T. Kelsey's *Dreams: A Way to Listen to God,* or his *God, Dreams, and Revelation: A Christian Interpretation of Dreams.*

12. Two of the best are *Jungian Dream Interpretation,* by James Hall, and *Dreams: A Portal to the Source,* by Edward Whitmont and Sylvia Perera.

13. While the woman in this fairy tale appears to be the greedy person and the fisherman looks innocent, in fact, from a psychological point of view, the fisherman's wife represents the man's anima, or feminine side, which can become an insatiable driving power complex in him. See my book *The Invisible Partners: How the Male and Female in Each of Us Affects Our Relationships.*

14. C. G. Jung, *Dream Analysis,* p. 77.

15. Ibid.

16. Sophocles, *Oedipus the King*, lines 872–882.

17. Aeschylus, *The Eumenides*, lines 526–537.

18. Aeschylus, *Agamemnon*, lines 763–771.

19. Samuel G. Green, *Handbook to the Grammar of the Greek New Testament*, p. 381.

20. Walter F. Otto, *The Homeric Gods*, p. 77.

21. Aeschylus, *Agamemnon*, lines 1194–1197.

22. Sophocles, *Oedipus at Colonus*, lines 960–968.

23. See S. H. Butcher, *Aristotle's Theory of Poetry and the Fine Arts*, pp. 317–323.

24. Euripides, *Hippolytus*, lines 1325, 1334–1335.

25. Confucius, *Doctrine of the Mean*, 14.5.

26. C. G. Jung, *Dream Analysis*, p. 90.

Conclusion

1. Aeschylus, *Agamemnon*, lines 176–180.

2. For the works of Kunkel, see my edited volume *Fritz Kunkel: Selected Writings*. A convenient summary of Kunkel's thought can be found in chapter 3, "The Tyranny of the Ego," in *What Men Are Like*, by John A. Sanford and George Lough.

Works Cited

Aeschylus. *Agamemnon*. Loeb Classical Library. 1983.
———. *The Eumenides*. Loeb Classical Library. 1983.
Berdyaev, Nicholas. *The Meaning of the Creative Act*. Trans. Donald A. Lowrie. New York: Harper & Brothers, n.d.
The Book of Common Prayer and Administration of the Sacraments and Other Rites and Ceremonies of the Church According to the Use of the Protestant Episcopal Church in the United States of America. New York: Seabury Press, 1928.
Butcher, S. H. *Aristotle's Theory of Poetry and the Fine Arts*. Dover edition. 1907.
Clement of Alexandria. *The Stromata*. In *The Ante-Nicene Fathers*, edited by Alexander Roberts and James Donaldson. Grand Rapids, Mich.: Wm. B. Eerdmans, 1957.
Concise Encyclopedia of Psychology. Edited by Raymond J. Corsini. New York: John Wiley & Sons, 1987.
Confucius. *The Doctrine of the Mean*. In *Confucian Analects, The Great Learning and The Doctrine of the Mean*. Trans. James Legge. New York: Dover Publications, 1971.

de Broglie, Louis, Louis Armand, Pierre-Henri Simon, et al., *Einstein.* New York: Peebles Press International, 1979.

Dodds, Eric Robertson. *The Greeks and the Irrational.* Boston: Beacon Press, 1957.

Dostoevsky, Fyodor. *Crime and Punishment.* Trans. Constance Garnett. Reprint. New York: Modern Library, 1950.

Euripides. *Hippolytus.* Loeb Classical Library. 1980.

"The Fisherman and His Wife." No. 103, Grimm's Fairy Tales. New York: Pantheon Books, 1972.

Freud, Sigmund. *The Interpretation of Dreams.* 1900. Reprint. New York: Modern Library, 1950.

Green, Samuel G. *Handbook to the Grammar of the Greek New Testament.* New York: Fleming H. Revell Co., 1912.

Gregory of Nyssa. Vol. 5, *Nicene and Post-Nicene Fathers of the Christian Church.* Series 2. Edited by Philip Schaff and Henry Wace. Grand Rapids: Wm. B. Eerdmans, n.d.

Hall, James. *Jungian Dream Interpretation.* Toronto: Inner City Books, 1983.

Harrison, Jane. *Prolegomena to the Study of Greek Religion.* New York: Meridian Books, 1960.

Homer. *The Odyssey.* Loeb Classical Library. 1984.

Jung, Carl Gustav. *Aion: Researches into the Phenomenology of the Self.* 2d ed. Vol. 9, pt. 2, *Collected Works.* Edited by Sir Herbert Read et al. Translated by R. F. C. Hull. Bollingen Series 20, no. 9. Princeton, N.J.: Princeton University Press, 1968.

———. *Answer to Job.* Translated by R. F. C. Hull. London: Routledge and Kegan Paul, 1954.

———. *Civilization in Transition.* Vol. 10, *Collected Works.* Edited by Sir Herbert Read et al. Translated by R. F. C. Hull. Bollingen Series 20, no. 10. New York: Pantheon Books, 1964.

———. *Dream Analysis.* Edited by William McGuire. Bollingen Series 99. Princeton, N.J.: Princeton University Press, 1984.

———. *Memories, Dreams, Reflections.* Edited by Aniela Jaffé.

Translated by Richard Winston and Clara Winston. New York: Pantheon Books, 1961.

———. *Psychology and Religion: West and East.* 2d ed. Vol. 11, *Collected Works.* Edited by Sir Herbert Read et al. Translated by R. F. C. Hull. Bollingen Series 20, no. 11. Princeton, N.J.: Princeton University Press, 1969.

———. "Yoga and the West," in *Psychology and Religion: West and East.* 2d ed. Vol. 11, *Collected Works.* Princeton, N.J.: Princeton University Press, 1969.

Kafka, Franz. *The Trial.* New York: Alfred A. Knopf, 1937.

Kelsey, Morton T. *Dreams: A Way to Listen to God.* New York: Paulist Press, 1978.

———. *God, Dreams, and Revelation: A Christian Interpretation of Dreams.* Minneapolis: Augsburg Publishing House, 1968.

———. *The Other Side of Silence: A Guide to Christian Meditation.* Ramsey, N.J.: Paulist/Newman Press, 1976.

Kluger, Rivkah Schärf. *Satan in the Old Testament.* Translated by Hildegard Nagel. Evanston, Ill.: Northwestern University Press, 1967.

Kunkel, Fritz. *Fritz Kunkel: Selected Writings.* Edited by John A. Sanford. Ramsey, N.J.: Paulist Press, 1984.

———. *In Search of Maturity: An Inquiry Into Psychology, Religion, and Self-Education.* New York: Charles Scribner's Sons, 1943.

L'Heureux, Conrad E. *Life Journey and the Old Testament: An Experiential Approach to the Bible and Personal Transformation.* Mahwah, N.J.: Paulist Press, 1986.

Lynch, James, M.D. *The Broken Heart: The Medical Consequences of Loneliness.* New York: Basic Books, 1977.

Otto, Walter F. *The Homeric Gods: The Spiritual Significance of Greek Religion.* Translated by Moses Hadas. New York: Thames and Hudson, 1954.

Plato, *Apology.* Loeb Classical Library. 1982.

Sanford, John A. *Dreams and Healing.* New York: Paulist Press, 1978.

————. *The Invisible Partners: How the Male and Female in Each of Us Affects Our Relationships*. New York: Paulist Press, 1980.

————. *The Kingdom Within: The Inner Meaning of Jesus' Sayings*. New York: Harper & Row, 1987.

————. *Soul Journey: A Jungian Analyst Looks at Reincarnation*. New York: Crossroad, 1991.

Sanford, John A., and George Lough. *What Men Are Like*. Mahwah, N.J.: Paulist Press, 1988.

Sophocles. *Antigone*. Loeb Classical Library. 1981.

————. *Oedipus at Colonus*. Loeb Classical Library. 1981.

————. *Oedipus the King*. Loeb Classical Library. 1981.

Tertullian. *Against Marcion*. In *Latin Christianity: Its Founder, Tertullian*. Vol. 3, *The Ante-Nicene Fathers*. Edited by Alexander Roberts and James Donaldson. Grand Rapids: Wm. B. Eerdmans Publishing Co., 1957.

Theissen, Gerd. *Psychological Aspects of Pauline Theology*. Translated by John P. Galvin. Philadelphia: Fortress Press, 1987.

Whitmont, Edward, and Sylvia Perera. *Dreams, A Portal to the Source: A Guide to Dream Interpretation*. New York: Routledge, 1989.

Whyte, Lancelot Law. *The Unconscious Before Freud: A History of the Evolution of Human Awareness*. New York: Basic Books, 1960.

Wilde, Oscar. *The Picture of Dorian Gray*. Yonkers, N.Y.: World Book Co., 1946.